RULING YOUR WORLD

McDougal & Associates
Servants of Christ and Stewards of the Mysteries of God

RULING YOUR WORLD

by

Dr. Abiola Idowu

Ruling Your World
Copyright © 2024—Abiola Idowu
ALL RIGHTS RESERVED

Unless otherwise noted, all Scripture references are from the *Holy Bible, King James Version*, public domain. References marked "AMPC" are from *The Amplified Bible*, Classic Edition, copyright © 1954, 1958, 1962, 1964, 1965, 1987 by The Lockman Foundation, La Habra, California. References marked "AMP" are from *The Amplified Bible*, copyright © 2015 by The Lockman Foundation, La Habra, California. References marked "NLT" are from *The New Living Translation of the Bible,* copyright © 1996 by Tyndale House Publishers, Inc., Wheaton, Illinois. References marked "MSG" are from *The Message*, copyright © 1993, 1994, 1995, 1996, 2000, 2002 by NavPress Publishing Group, Colorado Springs, Colorado. References marked "TPT" are from *The Passion Translation®*, copyright © 2017 by BroadStreet Publishing® Group, LLC. All rights reserved. Used by permission.

Published by:

McDougal & Associates
www.ThePublishedWord.com

McDougal & Associates is dedicated to spreading the Gospel of the Lord Jesus Christ to as many people as possible in the shortest time possible.

ISBN: 978-1-964665-09-2

Printed on demand in the U.S., the U.K., and Australia
For Worldwide Distribution

Dedication

This book is dedicated to Kingdom citizens, those who are born to rule the Earth as ambassadors of Christ. May the grace of the Lord Jesus Christ and the true knowledge of God multiply over your life.

Contents

Introduction 9

1. Understanding the God of New Things 13
2. Having Faith for New Things 50
3. Ruling Your World 90
4. Discovering Covenant Access 122
5. Securing Your Future 155
6. Unlocking Limitless Wonders 189
7. Walking in the Miraculous 229

Other Books by Dr. Abiola Idowu 277
Author Contact Information 181

> **The LORD shall send the rod of Your strength out of Zion. Rule in the midst of Your enemies!**
>
> — Psalm 110:2, NKJV

Introduction

It's interesting to know that God made this Earth for man, not for the angels, not for Satan, and not even for Himself:

> *The heaven, even the heavens, are the Lord's: but the earth hath he given to the children of men.* Psalm 115:16

Here on Earth, you are in your territory manifesting your God-given mandate. Many times, a lack of concise revelation knowledge of the Word of God regarding religion and popular culture has robbed us of our inheritance and made us slaves in what should be our domain.

The mandate of God to rule the Earth was part of the Creation Manual, and it cannot ever be changed. God gave the day for the sun to shine on and the night for the moon to dominate, and He gave to man the privilege and responsibility of subduing the Earth and ruling over it.

Why are we not ruling as God intended? The enemy set us up by lying to us and deceiving us the same way he deceived Adam and Eve. He convinced us that we are not good enough to rule. God shows us, however, that everything He created is already under our feet, and that includes the devil himself:

> *What is man, that thou art mindful of him? and the son of man, that thou visitest him? For thou hast made him a little lower than the angels, and hast crowned him with glory and honour. Thou madest him to have dominion over the works of thy hands; thou hast put all things under his feet.* Psalm 8:4-6

When a child of God lacks a basic understanding of what Jesus Christ did to bring restoration to our humanity, he then subjects

Introduction

himself to the torments of the wicked one through lies, misinformation, misinterpretation, and deception. How sad, for you were placed here to rule the Earth on God's behalf.

But you can't rule your world with the mindset of the world. There is a higher way of thinking and living that can set you over the affairs and operations of this world. No matter how smart you are, you cannot rule the world using the same system the world controls. You can only rule your world when you have moved into a higher realm of operations. That's what Jesus Christ came to preach, and He lived by it.

When you begin to use Kingdom principles and Kingdom systems, this world will have to bow to you. This will not be done through your own efforts; it will be effortless through the grace of God. That is why Jesus said:

> *Unto you it is given to know the mystery of the kingdom of God: but unto them that are without, all these things are done in parables.* Mark 4:11

This is a mystery that the human mind cannot understand or comprehend. God wants to reveal it to you so that the world will marvel at what He does through you.

There is no logical explanation for the conception of Jesus through Mary. The Word of God came to her, and she got pregnant. This shows that there will be no barren situation anywhere on Earth if the Word of God is embraced and received by faith. This book is all about taking your territory through Kingdom principles. Your openness to God's Word can bring about the recovery of everything you have lost.

Now, let's get into the truth of our divine mandate and adventure into the world of God through these pages. Your life will never be the same again. I commend you to God and to the Word of His grace that is able to build you up and give you your inheritance in the name of Jesus Christ. Shalom!

Dr. Abiola Idowu
Presiding Bishop CREPA worldwide

Chapter 1

Understanding the God of New Things

Then He who sat on the throne said, "Behold, I make all things new." And He said to me, "Write, for these words are true and faithful."
                    Revelation 21:5, NKJV

New things have always been on the agenda of God Almighty. From the beginning, everything was programmed to be new every day. But, because our minds are tied to old "stuff," they cannot see the new things that God has promised. He said, *"Behold, I make all things new."* Until you see it, you can't have it.

God's determination to raise a family on Earth to Himself through Christ speaks volumes. It was to be a family of results, a family of wonders, a family that provoked envy in others. It was to be a royal family, a family of new things. Our world had never seen a family like this one, and it all starts with a new creation:

> *Therefore if any man be in Christ, he is a new creature: old things are passed away; behold, all things are become new. And all things are of God, who hath reconciled us to himself by Jesus Christ, and hath given to us the ministry of reconciliation.* 2 Corinthians 5:17-18

We are directly connected to Heaven in order to make unusual waves here on Earth. You are not common at all. Why? Because you are connected to Christ, and He that is from above is above all:

> *Jesus answered him, "I assure you and most solemnly say to you, unless*

a person is born again [reborn from above—spiritually transformed, renewed, sanctified], he cannot [ever] see and experience the kingdom of God."
John 3:3, AMP

We are the children that have access to the bread and not the crumbs (see Mark 7:27-28). You are not here to suffer at all, so don't opt for that. The secret of our fruitfulness is that we are so filled with all the fullness of Christ (see Ephesians 3:19) that it makes it impossible for us not to produce results.

Let's look at Isaiah 43 again:

Behold, I will do a new thing; now it shall spring forth; shall ye not know it? I will even make a way in the wilderness, and rivers in the desert. The beast of the field shall honour me, the dragons and the owls: because I give waters in the wilderness, and rivers in the desert, to give drink to my people, my chosen.
Isaiah 43:19-20

The way God sees things is completely different from the way man sees them, and the good news is this: the way God views things is far greater and better than the way man sees them. He sees things from an eternal point of view, a love point of view, a purpose point of view. He said, *"Behold, I will do a new thing, now it shall spring forth."* Believe it!

Every new thing that God manifests in our lives comes with a new mindset. To make it work, you have to come on board and think the Bible way. You cannot have a new mindset and not turn to a new way of life. If you can't see it, you can't think it, and if you can't think it, you can't enjoy it. God said it, so start experiencing it. *"Behold, I will do a new thing."*

New things are great, but they must be seen by vision. If you have no vision, all that God is set to do in your life becomes meaningless. Israel saw a bunch of grasshoppers, but God saw kings and priests. The generation that left Egypt died without realizing God's plan because of their spiritual

Understanding the God of New Things

blindness. When God says, *"I will do a new thing,"* let's see what is in His mind and then flow with it.

New things start with *"I will make a way."* The reason so many people are stagnated and depressed in life is that they don't know the way forward. The door seems closed to them. When this is true, it takes a great deal of expectation on your part to know that God will come through for you. But you can't be held bound in that situation any longer. A jealous God is coming for you now. He said, *"I will make a way in the wilderness,"* He is the Almighty, and making a way in difficult places is easy for Him.

Jeremiah proclaimed:

> *Ah Lord God! behold, thou hast made the heaven and the earth by thy great power and stretched out arm, and there is nothing too hard for thee.*
> Jeremiah 32:17

The place between where you are and where you are going is called *wilderness*, and the frustrating thing is that not everyone gets out of their wilderness before they die. Why? Because they don't know the God of new things and how He operates. The principles of God are there, and the testimonies of God prove that you're next. He is a specialist in new things, bringing new order and new results.

Everyone said that Elizabeth was barren, but God didn't agree. He said to Mary, her cousin:

> *And, behold, thy cousin Elisabeth, she hath also conceived a son in her old age: and this is the sixth month with her, who was called barren. For with God nothing shall be impossible.*
>
> Luke 1:36-37

Men said she was barren, but they were not God. If you stick to God's Word, men's conclusions about you will be proved wrong. Whatever has been said about you that is not from God. Let it drop off of you today. He said, *"I will make a way,"* and He

Understanding the God of New Things

will, if you will believe Him and cooperate with the process.

When unusual opportunities open to you, that is God making a way. A group of sons of the prophets went with Elisha to cut down trees to expand their dwelling place. Unfortunately the head of the axe one of them was using came off and fell into the water. Alarmed, he cried out: *Alas, master! For it was borrowed"* (2 Kings 6:5, NKJV). What were they to do now?

The man of God knew that when a thing is irretrievable, that's when God can step in with a miracle. He asked, *"Where did it fall?"* (Verse 6, NKJV). When the younger man showed him the spot where the axe head fell, *"he cut off a stick, and threw it in there; and he made the iron float. Therefore he said, 'Pick it up for yourself.' So he reached out his hand and took it"* (Verses 6-7).

That same God is ready to do miracles for you today. May everything that has been lost in your life come swimming back to you in the matchless name of Jesus. God has not changed, and He said, *"I will make a way."*

What happens when God makes a way?

1. WHEN GOD MAKES A WAY, YOU EXPERIENCE SUPERNATURAL FAVOR

> *So the LORD said, "I will destroy man whom I have created from the face of the earth, both man and beast, creeping thing and birds of the air, for I am sorry that I have made them." But Noah found grace in the eyes of the LORD.*
> Genesis 6:7-8, NKJV

No matter what kills others, you are exempt. It's called favor. Even when a verdict has been pronounced, you find favor.

The qualification for Noah's favor was that he was righteous:

> *Then the LORD said to Noah, "Come into the ark, you and all your household, because I have seen that you are righteous before Me in this generation."*
> Genesis 7:1, NKJV

But you, dear reader, are righteous too:

For He made Him who knew no sin to be sin for us, that we might become the righteousness of God in Him.
2 Corinthians 5:21, NKJV

When Noah was in the ark, none of the animals could hurt him—snakes, lions, even germs. The ark floated as every other living thing on Earth died in the flood. Beloved, you are in the living Ark, Jesus Christ, the Son of God. He said:

These things I have spoken to you, that in Me you may have peace.
John 16:33, NKJV

In Christ, there is no labor and no burden, only total freedom. Covid-19 is dead as far as you are concerned, in Jesus' name. If you have sensed a burden, then cast it on Jesus now. He will bear it for you.

When Noah got inside that ark, God shut the door, and nothing and no one could come in. In Christ Jesus, no evil can come your way again.

2. WHEN GOD MAKES A WAY, THE ENEMY IS DISAPPOINTED

"For Pharaoh will say of the children of Israel, 'They are bewildered by the land; the wilderness has closed them in.' Then I will harden Pharaoh's heart, so that he will pursue them; and I will gain honor over Pharaoh and over all his army, that the Egyptians may know that I am the LORD.'" And they did so.
Exodus 14:3-4, NKJV

The world can't pull you down, no matter how much it tries. Pharaoh was sure the people of God were *"closed in."* "Let's go get them," he said with obvious delight, but the next thing he knew, he, along with his great army, were all drowning in the Red Sea. May every evil that has targeted your life be drowned today in the name of Jesus Christ.

Understanding the God of New Things

In Esther's time, all of the people of Israel had been assigned to die. The documents had been sealed by the king's signet. That was the moment when the God of Heaven and Earth stepped in. Not everyone was so sure about the defeat of God's people:

> *When Haman told his wife Zeresh and all his friends everything that had happened to him, his wise men and his wife Zeresh said to him, "If Mordecai, before whom you have begun to fall, is of Jewish descent, you will not prevail against him but will surely fall before him."* Esther 6:13, NKJV

For some odd reason, King Ahasuerus could not sleep that night, and the result was that the judgement was reversed. Every judgement against your destiny is reversed now in Jesus' name.

God said it in Isaiah 54:17:

> *"No weapon formed against you shall prosper,*

*And every tongue which rises against
you in judgment
You shall condemn.
This is the heritage of the servants of
the LORD,
And their righteousness is from Me,"
Says the LORD.* (NKJV)

Who will you believe?

3. WHEN GOD MAKES A WAY, WHAT KILLS OTHERS CANNOT KILL YOU

*For the LORD's portion is His people;
Jacob is the place of His inheritance.
He found him in a desert land
And in the wasteland, a howling wilderness;
He encircled him, He instructed him,
He kept him as the apple of His eye.
As an eagle stirs up its nest,
Hovers over its young,
Spreading out its wings, taking them up,
Carrying them on its wings,*
              Deuteronomy 32:9-11, NKJV

When all of Egypt went dark, the children of Israel had light in their dwellings:

> *They did not see one another; nor did anyone rise from his place for three days. But all the children of Israel had light in their dwellings.* Exodus 10:23, NKJV

When Paul was bitten by a very venomous snake, those who witnessed it expected him to quickly swell up and die. Their expectations were dashed:

> *And when the barbarians saw the venomous beast hang on his hand, they said among themselves, No doubt this man is a murderer, whom, though he hath escaped the sea, yet vengeance suffereth not to live. And he shook off the beast into the fire, and felt no harm. Howbeit they looked when he should have swollen, or fallen down dead suddenly: but after they had looked a great while, and saw no harm come to him, they changed their minds, and said that he was a god.* Acts 28:4-6

When you are in Christ, the people around you will change their minds about you and your future too.

4. WHEN GOD MAKES A WAY, YOU CANNOT BE STOPPED OR HINDERED

> *"Enlarge the place of your tent,*
> *And let them stretch out the curtains of your dwellings;*
> *Do not spare;*
> *Lengthen your cords,*
> *And strengthen your stakes.*
> *For you shall expand to the right and to the left,*
> *And your descendants will inherit the nations,*
> *And make the desolate cities inhabited.*
> Isaiah 54:2-3, NKJV

Lift up your heads, O you gates!
And be lifted up, you everlasting doors!
And the King of glory shall come in.
Who is this King of glory?
The LORD strong and mighty,

> *The LORD mighty in battle.*
> *Lift up your heads, O you gates!*
> *Lift up, you everlasting doors!*
> *And the King of glory shall come in.*
>
> Psalm 24:7-9, NKJV

That says it all. God can do it, but you must commit to Him. How do we commit to God?

1. BELIEVE HIS WORD

There is no room for new things if God's Word is not honored and put in its rightful place. It was by the Word that everything that exists was created. You don't have to analyze it; you just need to believe it and act on it.

Jairus, the ruler of the synagogue, had heard of Jesus and was seeking His help for a daughter who was gravely ill. While he was still with Jesus, someone from his house came and delivered some tragic news:

> *"Your daughter is dead. Why trouble the Teacher any further?"*
>
> Mark 5:35, NKJV

But Jesus didn't agree:

> *As soon as Jesus heard the word that was spoken, He said to the ruler of the synagogue, "Do not be afraid; only believe."* Verse 36, NKJV

"*Only believe!*" Believe what? Jairus had to believe that Jesus was there with him, and he had just witnessed Jesus healing a woman who had long suffered an issue of blood. His issue would be resolved too, and your issues can be settled as you believe today.

When Lazarus had died, Jesus told his sister Martha:

> *"Did I not say to you that if you would believe you would see the glory of God?"* John 11:40, NKJV

"*If you would believe ...*" Believe what? Believe that He was the resurrection and the life. Believe that He was the Living Word and that He would make a way. Oh, thank You, Jesus. Make a way now for us—physically, spiritually, and financially. Yes, my way is made. Hallelujah!

2. Declare His Word

Every time you declare the Word, you settle that Word here on Earth. The Word is settled in Heaven waiting for your agreement. The biblical rule is this:

> *By the mouth of two or three witnesses every word may be established.*
> Matthew 18:16, NKJV

Heaven has already established it, and you must agree with it now to make two witnesses.

As a child of God, your words are powerful:

> *For assuredly, I say to you, whoever says to this mountain, "Be removed and be cast into the sea," and does not doubt in his heart, but believes that those things he says will be done, he will have whatever he says.* Mark 11:23, NKJV

"Whatever he says." It was the agreement of Mary that brought about the conception of Jesus. Agree with God now, and see what marvels He will do for you.

3. SEE THE WAY GOD SEES

If you can't see what God sees, you cannot operate in His realm. God speaks based on what He sees. He saw Abraham as a father of nations when, in the earthly reality, the man was very old and had a barren wife. God said to him:

> *No longer shall your name be called Abram, but your name shall be Abraham; for I have made you a father of many nations.* Genesis 17:5, NKJV

Even though Abraham was so old (his natural ability to produce was gone) and Sarah was barren, he was able to see himself as God saw him. If you don't see what He sees, you will doubt Him and miss your miracle.

God saw a Messiah forming in the womb of Mary, and she saw it too:

And Mary said, Behold the handmaid of the Lord; be it unto me according to thy word. And the angel departed from her. Luke 1:38

What are you seeing? The Word of God is true. See it and own it!

4. Be Kingdom Minded and Committed

Membership is different from citizenship. Members are not always great. They are made up of cells, and cells die and are replaced, but citizenship is eternal and it's a responsibility. Be a citizen of the Kingdom and be responsible.

There is nothing you need in life that is not available to you now. All that is needed is your commitment to Kingdom business. All that God wants to do with your destiny is subjective to you committing to the Kingdom.

Jesus said:

Ruling Your World

> *But seek ye first the kingdom of God, and his righteousness; and all these things shall be added unto you.*
> Matthew 6:33

"All these things!"

- Father, I give You thanks and praise for Your goodness and mercies over my life. You are gracious. Thank You for Your New-Things Agenda in my life
- Father, in the name of Jesus Christ, I agree with You now. New things, begin to manifest in my life—physically, spiritually, and financially.
- Father, in the name of Jesus Christ, a great way is open to me the remaining days of this year in Jesus' name.
- Father, in the name of Jesus Christ, let every way You have made for me manifest physically now in Jesus' name.
- Father, in the name of Jesus Christ, every adversary of my new things are removed permanently now in Jesus' name.

Understanding the God of New Things

God says to you today:

"I will establish you. Mighty doors will open, strange opportunities. I will untie everyone that is held down. There will be liberty everywhere," says the Lord.

Isaiah declared:

Instead of shame and dishonor,
  you will enjoy a double share of honor.
You will possess a double portion of prosperity in your land,
  and everlasting joy will be yours.
                    Isaiah 61:7, NLT

God is digging into every area of your life right now. Whatever is not glorifying Him shall be removed in Jesus' name. The fire of God is set on every corner of your concerns this day, and they shall be burned up.

I heard the word *why*? Everything planted or growing in the wrong place is being removed now. There shall be peace and beauty.

Isaiah recorded God's promise:

> *And in this mountain shall the LORD of hosts make unto all people a feast of fat things, a feast of wines on the lees, of fat things full of marrow, of wines on the lees well refined. And he will destroy in this mountain the face of the covering cast over all people, and the vail that is spread over all nations. He will swallow up death in victory; and the LORD God will wipe away tears from off all faces; and the rebuke of his people shall he take away from off all the earth: for the LORD hath spoken it.*
> Isaiah 25:6-8

When you know the heart of Jesus Christ, you will be able to believe God for anything and will know that there is no limitations for you in life. Jesus said:

> *Ask, using my name, and you will receive, and you will have abundant joy.*
> John 16:24, NLT

With all the disciples had experienced, Jesus said, *"Hitherto have ye asked nothing in my name"* (Same verse). There is something very important here that I want you to see:

> *Whosoever is born of God doth not commit sin; for his seed remaineth in him: and he cannot sin, because he is born of God.*   1 John 3:9

God's seed is inside of us, and that seed will germinate and produce a harvest that will cause others to envy you. I'm not only talking about physical results but also a great spiritual impact.

God's seed doesn't die. This brings hope and confidence that we are fully in charge of life in and through Christ Jesus. As long as that seed is inside of us, the future is secure.

It is true that Jesus Christ is coming back, and we are awaiting His arrival. But the sons and daughters of God must manifest first before the coming of our King:

> *For the earnest expectation of the creature waiteth for the manifestation of the sons of God.* Romans 8:19

God's Word is true, so stop believing a lie. Lies will only end in delusion. God is true and in Him there is no deceit.

We are putting on the glory of Heaven and manifesting His power now on Earth. Nothing can stop the will of God in your life except you. God's will is as powerful as His Person. It forms the foundation of His Kingdom:

> *So shall my word be that goeth forth out of my mouth: it shall not return unto me void, but it shall accomplish that which I please, and it shall prosper in the thing whereto I sent it.* Isaiah 55:11

God's will is to do a new thing, and He is set to do it if you will obey His rules. Spiritual laws are powerful and indestructible, and they work, if you work them. The same power that transforms a child of the

Understanding the God of New Things

devil into a child of God is available to make all things new for you today. God said, *"I will even make a way in the wilderness, and rivers in the desert."* This is His way of doing new things. He brings water in unusual places. He will not only make a way; He will bring provisions and quench your thirst.

God is not in the business of refurbishing; He's all about new things. He will fill you with the Holy Spirit and make you extraordinary among men.

We're not here just for small springs of water; we want the rivers. God has declared Himself; now the rest is up to you. Great accomplishments are possible in Christ through the ministry of the Holy Spirit. His water poured inside of you will make you do extraordinary things:

> *In the last day, that great day of the feast, Jesus stood and cried, saying, If any man thirst, let him come unto me, and drink. He that believeth on me, as the scripture hath said, out of his belly shall flow rivers of living water. (But*

> *this spake he of the Spirit, which they that believe on him should receive: for the Holy Ghost was not yet given; because that Jesus was not yet glorified.)*
> John 7:37-39

> *Verily, verily, I say unto you, He that believeth on me, the works that I do shall he do also; and greater works than these shall he do; because I go unto my Father.* John 14:12

God makes everything new, and as His saints, we can receive fresh and new things from Heaven every day. Our teaming up with God and accepting the help of the Holy Ghost is key to us walking in the realm of wonders. Jesus said:

> *Howbeit when he, the Spirit of truth, is come, he will guide you into all truth: for he shall not speak of himself; but whatsoever he shall hear, that shall he speak: and he will shew you things to come.* John 16:13. KJV

Understanding the God of New Things

You are never out of information when God's Spirit dwells in you. The King on the inside of you is crowned for reigning, and you, too, can reign in life when the Holy Ghost comes over you and empowers you.

When He comes, you have come to the end of your hunger and thirst. Now your every need will be supplied. No more drought! You will be fruitful. Through the Holy Spirit you are connected with surprises. You can't see them yet, but they *will* come.

You will now thrive where others are dying and struggling:

> *When men are cast down, then thou shalt say, There is lifting up; and he shall save the humble person.*
>
> Job 22:29

You will be like a tree planted by the rivers of water:

> *And he shall be like a tree planted by the rivers of water, that bringeth forth his fruit in his season; his leaf also shall not*

> *wither; and whatsoever he doeth shall prosper.* Psalm 1:3

"*Whatsoever!*" Believe it today. These rivers bring life:

> *And it shall come to pass, that every thing that liveth, which moveth, whithersoever the rivers shall come, shall live: and there shall be a very great multitude of fish, because these waters shall come thither: for they shall be healed; and every thing shall live whither the river cometh.* Ezekiel 47:9

With God on your side, you are the envy of your world, for no one else can produce the same kinds of results:

> *Then Isaac sowed in that land, and received in the same year an hundredfold: and the* L<small>ORD</small> *blessed him. And the man waxed great, and went forward, and grew until he became very great: for he had possession of flocks, and possession*

of herds, and great store of servants: and the Philistines envied him.
                              Genesis 26:12-14

You constantly have fresh ideas and are growing in every way. If that all sounds good to you, let me give you some keys to make this kind of godly favor flow in your life.

1. WALK IN WISDOM

The end-time church will be winning life's battles and conquering by the practical application of the wisdom of God, which the world cannot comprehend:

> *To the intent that now unto the principalities and powers in heavenly places might be known by the church the manifold wisdom of God.* Ephesians 3:10

This will draw the attention of the world to the Church:

Ruling Your World

> *And it shall come to pass in the last days, that the mountain of the LORD's house shall be established in the top of the mountains, and shall be exalted above the hills; and all nations shall flow unto it.* Isaiah 2:2

> *Who are these that fly as a cloud, and as the doves to their windows?*
> Isaiah 60:8

God's people will be high flyers. Why? Because He is bringing water to their deserts. The world is crying, but they are flying. It's called wisdom. It comes by taking the Word of God literally and acting on it while the world is busy analyzing and debating it.

How can we possibly explain Paul's snake bite? He just shook the beast off into the fire and felt no hurt. The result was that the local people called him a god:

> *Howbeit they looked when he should have swollen, or fallen down dead*

> *suddenly: but after they had looked a great while, and saw no harm come to him, they changed their minds, and said that he was a god.* Acts 28:6

Why did they call him a god? Because the life of God was inside of him. God said:

> *By me kings reign, and princes decree justice.* Proverbs 8:15

You and I are redeemed to become kings, and God's wisdom is our identity. How could Adam rule the Earth? Because his Father was the all-wise God, and they walked and talked together every day:

> *He that walketh with wise men shall be wise: but a companion of fools shall be destroyed.* Proverbs 13:20

Because Adam was walking with the all-wise God, he was able to share that wisdom and, with it, rule the planet.

God's wisdom is enshrouded in His Word, and the presence of the Holy Spirit inside of you is the key to interpreting that Word. A wise man hears or reads the Word and then does it.

The resources of the Earth cannot be harnessed and put to use without the wisdom of God:

> *And Adam said, This is now bone of my bones, and flesh of my flesh: she shall be called Woman, because she was taken out of Man.* Genesis 2:23

How did Adam know that Eve was bone of his bones? It's called wisdom, and it only comes from God Almighty. A magnitude of wisdom has been restored back to man through our Lord Jesus Christ. God made Jesus to us wisdom, Jesus, the Word of God. God's wisdom is His equipment for supernatural manifestation. Get it and use it well!

2. BE EXPECTANT

Understanding the God of New Things

Without expectation, faith is dead. Without expectation, there is no manifestation. Having an expectation is the proof that you know God will show up for you and your situation.

For surely there is an end; and thine expectation shall not be cut off.
                                                           Proverbs 23:18

Expectation is a product of trust and positive anticipation. It increases your enthusiasm and confidence. If I were to say to you, "I will be giving you a large check tomorrow by 2 PM, it would set your expectations, and you would probably arrive at my house before that time. Why? Because you knew I wouldn't lie about a thing like that.

God wants you to be expectant that your deserts are being turned into cities. He said, *"I will do a new thing now."* If you believe it, it will produce an expectation and cause you to prepare for it.

It's like a pregnant woman. She is expecting, so she prepares for the coming of the baby. She can't hold it in her arms yet, but she knows that day is comig. When your expectations are from God, the enemy is doomed. Why? Because he can't stop what you are believing for from happening. Only you can do that:

> *My soul, wait thou only upon God; for my expectation is from him. He only is my rock and my salvation: he is my defence; I shall not be moved.*
>
> Psalm 62:5-6

If you know how big and powerful your Father is, you will expect great things from Him:

> *In the last day, that great day of the feast, Jesus stood and cried, saying, If any man thirst, let him come unto me, and drink. He that believeth on me, as the scripture hath said, out of his belly shall flow rivers of living water. (But this spake he of the Spirit, which they that believe on him should receive: for*

the Holy Ghost was not yet given; because that Jesus was not yet glorified.)
John 7:37-39

Our God can't stand anyone being hungry or thirsty. Come to Him with great expectation, change your posture, and expect your situation to change as well.

The crippled man at the Beautiful Gate was expectant, and he got much more than he expected. He was made whole. Jesus is right there with you this day. Be made whole! The provisions are there. Do you know they are for you? Then take what you need now in Jesus' name.

Don't do things just because other people are doing them. Do it with expectation.

3. Believe in the Ministry of Angels

There are places God knows you can't get to and things you can't achieve on your own. That's why He gave you servants to get you to your Promise Land without a struggle:

> *But to which of the angels said he at any time, Sit on my right hand, until I make thine enemies thy footstool? Are they not all ministering spirits, sent forth to minister for them who shall be heirs of salvation?* Hebrews 1:13-14

The journey to your Canaan can be stressful, and there are giants on the way, but no giant can stop an angel:

> *Bless the LORD, ye his angels, that excel in strength, that do his commandments, hearkening unto the voice of his word.*
> Psalm 103:20

The Bible says

> *Behold, I send an Angel before thee, to keep thee in the way, and to bring thee into the place which I have prepared.*
> Exodus 23:20

Angels will carry you in their hands lest you dash your foot against a stone:

Understanding the God of New Things

For he shall give his angels charge over thee, to keep thee in all thy ways. They shall bear thee up in their hands, lest thou dash thy foot against a stone.
                              Psalm 91:11-12

Angels are always there to get the job done. They act on the Word of God on your behalf. Believe for them and cooperate with them.

It is an impossible situation for a virgin to conceive and bear a child, but an angel took that message to Mary and got the job done. Your angel is ready to go to work for you in Jesus' name.

Yes, when you understand the God of new things, you can start *Ruling Your World.*

Chapter 2

Having Faith for New Things

According as his divine power hath given unto us all things that pertain unto life and godliness, through the knowledge of him that hath called us to glory and virtue: whereby are given unto us exceeding great and precious promises: that by these ye might be partakers of the divine nature, having escaped the corruption that is in the world through lust.   2 Peter 1:3-4

Everything that pertains to life and godliness has been purchased by Jesus Christ for you, but you will need faith to take it. Never

Having Faith for New Things

forget: there is nothing in the physical realm that does not have its root in the realm of the Spirit. The spirit realm is the manufacturing center, the production center for the physical realm. Tapping into the spiritual realm is called "faith." Why? Because this realm is not accessible to the human senses. In fact, there is no physical evidence that it even exists. It is faith that makes it real:

> *Now faith is the assurance (title deed, confirmation) of things hoped for (divinely guaranteed), and the evidence of things not seen [the conviction of their reality—faith comprehends as fact what cannot be experienced by the physical senses].* Hebrews 11:1, AMP

All you need to see into the spirit realm is faith in God. When you know, by faith, that God cannot lie, and you can begin to access and utilize the spirit realm, then you realize that God is more real than your physical senses.

The struggle of life ends when faith comes into operation. Why? Because faith honors

God, and whoever honors Him He will honor.

God honors faith. The evidence of faith is the Word of God. If you see something in the Word, you can have it in your daily life:

> *Then it happened, as He was coming near Jericho, that a certain blind man sat by the road begging. And hearing a multitude passing by, he asked what it meant. So they told him that Jesus of Nazareth was passing by. And he cried out, saying, "Jesus, Son of David, have mercy on me!"*
>
> *Then those who went before warned him that he should be quiet; but he cried out all the more, "Son of David, have mercy on me!"*
>
> *So Jesus stood still and commanded him to be brought to Him. And when he had come near, He asked him, saying, "What do you want Me to do for you?"*
>
> *He said, "Lord, that I may receive my sight."*

Then Jesus said to him, "Receive your sight; your faith has made you well." And immediately he received his sight, and followed Him, glorifying God. And all the people, when they saw it, gave praise to God. Luke 18:35-43, NKJV

What gave this man his sight? It was faith Jesus said. Jesus had sight, and this man's faith caused him to reach out and take what he needed from Jesus.

New things are a regular occurrence when our faith is alive. We don't have to be pitied by anyone. Put your faith to work, and get whatever you need today.

Here's another case:

When Jesus departed from there, two blind men followed Him, crying out and saying, "Son of David, have mercy on us!"
And when He had come into the house, the blind men came to Him. And Jesus said to them, "Do you believe that I am able to do this?"

> *They said to Him, "Yes, Lord."*
> *Then He touched their eyes, saying, "According to your faith let it be to you." And their eyes were opened. And Jesus sternly warned them, saying, "See that no one knows it." But when they had departed, they spread the news about Him in all that country.*
> Matthew 9:27-29, NKJV

Can you see how simple this was?
"Do you believe I can do this."
"Yes, Lord."
"Then be healed."
And it was so.

Do you believe that God can heal you? Then it will be done. *"According to your faith be it unto you."*

KNOW THAT GOD HAS NOT CHANGED

Faith is essential, and without it we cannot please God:

Having Faith for New Things

> *But without faith it is impossible to please him: for he that cometh to God must believe that he is, and that he is a rewarder of them that diligently seek him.* Hebrews 11:6

The foundation of our faith is based on the fact that God has not changed. He is more current than you or me, He is aware of what is going on in our lives, and He has the power to fix it. He fixed the life of Abraham, He fixed the life of Daniel and of so many others. As long as Daniel believed, no lion could swallow him.

Here's what Jesus said:

> *But Jesus answered them, My Father worketh hitherto, and I work.* John 5:17

All that is missing, then, is your faith. God is always at work on your behalf.

Know that God's Love for You Commits Him to Bless You

If you don't come to an understanding of the God dimension of love, it will be difficult to have faith in Him:

He that loveth not knoweth not God; for God is love.

And we have known and believed the love that God hath to us. God is love; and he that dwelleth in love dwelleth in God, and God in him.

1 John 4:8 and 16

Love endures long and is patient and kind; love never is envious nor boils over with jealousy, is not boastful or vainglorious, does not display itself haughtily. It is not conceited (arrogant and inflated with pride); it is not rude (unmannerly) and does not act unbecomingly. Love (God's love in us) does not insist on its own rights or its own way, for it is not self-seeking; it is not touchy or fretful or resentful; it takes no account of the evil done to it [it pays no attention to a suffered wrong]. It does not rejoice at injustice and unrighteousness, but rejoices when right and truth prevail. Love bears up under anything and everything that comes, is ever ready to believe the best

of every person, its hopes are fadeless under all circumstances, and it endures everything [without weakening].
                    1 Corinthians 13:4-7, AMPC

Love will do anything to get you blessed. It is not based on what you do but who He is:

The L<small>ORD</small> is compassionate and merciful, slow to get angry and filled with unfailing love.
He will not constantly accuse us, nor remain angry forever.
He does not punish us for all our sins; he does not deal harshly with us, as we deserve.
For his unfailing love toward those who fear him
is as great as the height of the Heavens above the earth.
He has removed our sins as far from us as the east is from the west.
The L<small>ORD</small> is like a father to his children, tender and compassionate to those who fear him.

For he knows how weak we are;
he remembers we are only dust.
Psalm 103:8-14, NLT

UNDERSTAND THAT THE COVENANT OF GOD WITH ABRAHAM IS A GUARANTEE THAT NEW THINGS MUST HAPPEN IN YOUR LIFE

What's more, I am changing your name. It will no longer be Abram. Instead, you will be called Abraham, for you will be the father of many nations.
Genesis 17:5, NLT

And now that you belong to Christ, you are the true children of Abraham. You are his heirs, and God's promise to Abraham belongs to you.
Galatians 3:29, NLT

And you, dear brothers and sisters, are children of the promise, just like Isaac.
Galatians 4:28, NLT

That promise includes you and me.

Understand that Things Not Changing Immediately Is Not an Indication that God Has Abandoned You

The trial of faith is not a denial of your blessing. In fact, it's just a preparation for a glorious future, that is if you will not quit. God allows our faith to be tried so that we can totally depend on Him:

> *For thou, O God, hast proved us: thou hast tried us, as silver is tried. Thou broughtest us into the net; thou laidst affliction upon our loins. Thou hast caused men to ride over our heads; we went through fire and through water: but thou broughtest us out into a wealthy place.* Psalm 66:10-12

When you abandon yourself to God and His Word, it's no more faith. Now it is called "trust." Job trusted God totally:

Though he slay me, yet will I trust in him: but I will maintain mine own ways before him. Job 13:15

Understand that Our redemption is the foundation for New Things in Our Lives

Therefore if any man be in Christ, he is a new creature: old things are passed away; behold, all things are become new. 2 Corinthians 5:17

In Christ, no one is permitted to fail or become obscure. You have been planted and watered, and now you must respond to see the glory of the Lord:

He spake also this parable; A certain man had a fig tree planted in his vineyard; and he came and sought fruit thereon, and found none. Then said he unto the dresser of his vineyard, Behold, these three years I come seeking fruit on this fig tree, and find none: cut it down;

why cumbereth it the ground? And he answering said unto him, Lord, let it alone this year also, till I shall dig about it, and dung it: and if it bear fruit, well: and if not, then after that thou shalt cut it down. Luke 13:6-9

UNDERSTAND THAT THE OLD THINGS ARE GONE

With the new birth, old things are gone. Stubbornly holding fast to them will reduce your impact. That doesn't mean that God is mad at you. Even when you were bad, He loved you. Now that you are saved, He anoints you, empowers you, and employs you:

For we are labourers together with God: ye are God's husbandry, ye are God's building. 1 Corinthians 3:9

Your life has not been structured to become stagnated. We are citizens of Heaven living on Earth, and as such, we must serve as examples. We are ambassadors and representatives of God down here.

Your office is enviable. If we are sent the same way Jesus was sent, then we are living wonders. What happens here does not entangle us, for we don't claim the citizenship of the Earth but of Heaven, and the government of Heaven takes our case.

Understand Your Value to God

But the very hairs of your head are all numbered. Fear ye not therefore, ye are of more value than many sparrows.
Matthew 10:30-31

You are valuable to God:

For ye are bought with a price: therefore glorify God in your body, and in your spirit, which are God's.
1 Corinthians 6:20

You are valued because the cost determines the value, and it took the life of God

Himself to get you back. You have been bought with a great price.

UNDERSTAND YOUR CALLING

Jesus said He was sending us out as sheep among wolves. But, He assured us, His wisdom would protect us. *"Be wise,"* He said:

> *Behold, I send you forth as sheep in the midst of wolves: be ye therefore wise as serpents, and harmless as doves.*
> Matthew 10:16

Because of our high calling, we have access to the same wisdom that made Jesus stand out:

> *And when the sabbath day was come, he began to teach in the synagogue: and many hearing him were astonished, saying, From whence hath this man these things? and what wisdom is this which is given unto him, that even*

> *such mighty works are wrought by his hands?* Mark 6:2

God has given us power, just as Jesus had power:

> *And when he had called unto him his twelve disciples, he gave them power against unclean spirits, to cast them out, and to heal all manner of sickness and all manner of disease.* Matthew 10:16

The manifestation of our redemption is all about the new mindset and not religiosity. As far as God is concerned, you are the victor in all things. Paul wrote:

> *But thanks be to God, which giveth us the victory through our Lord Jesus Christ.* 1 Corinthians 15:57

Satan is now the victim, and this verdict is eternal. God means what He says and says what He means. In Him, we are *"more than conquerors"*:

Having Faith for New Things

> *Nay, in all these things we are more than conquerors through him that loved us.* Romans 8:37

Yes, you are a new creation in Christ Jesus. Your mind and your environment may deceive you, but faith in what God says will give you the victory every time.

This knowledge makes you behave like God and reason like Him. Why? You now have God's nature, His life, and His power:

> *Ye have not chosen me, but I have chosen you, and ordained you, that ye should go and bring forth fruit, and that your fruit should remain: that whatsoever ye shall ask of the Father in my name, he may give it you.* John 15:16

In and through Christ Jesus, you now have dominion. This means you rule over a Kingdom domain where nothing is permitted to enter your territory without your permission.

Jesus said, *"Occupy till I come"*:

> *And he called his ten servants, and delivered them ten pounds, and said unto them, Occupy till I come.*
>
> Luke 19:13

Because the great I AM is in charge of all things, and I am His representative. Therefore, I am now in charge here. That is my assignment, and this mindset is the secret of new things in God's Kingdom:

> *Behold, I give unto you power to tread on serpents and scorpions, and over all the power of the enemy: and nothing shall by any means hurt you.*
>
> Luke 10:19

Why, then, do believers in Christ not measure up to these promises? I am convinced that the reason for every oppression is ignorance. Ignorance will kill faith and encourage fear. When we believe, it causes a revolution and an intimidation in the camp of the enemy.

Just as David said:

Thou preparest a table before me in the presence of mine enemies: thou anointest my head with oil; my cup runneth over. Psalm 23:5

UNDERSTAND THAT THE POWER OF SIN HAS BEEN DESTROYED

He that committeth sin is of the devil; for the devil sinneth from the beginning. For this purpose the Son of God was manifested, that he might destroy the works of the devil. 1 John 3:8

What does this mean? It means that Satan is no longer an issue, and if that is true, then failure is under arrest, along with sickness, disease, and premature death. Good-bye Covid-19! When we see the captive holding his master in bondage, we can know that it ought not to be. Shake yourself from the dust, *"O captive daughter of Zion"*:

Awake, awake; put on thy strength, O Zion; put on thy beautiful garments, O

Ruling Your World

> *Jerusalem, the holy city: for henceforth there shall no more come into thee the uncircumcised and the unclean. Shake thyself from the dust; arise, and sit down, O Jerusalem: loose thyself from the bands of thy neck, O captive daughter of Zion.* Isaiah 52:1-2

Declare your emancipation now! Enough, Satan! Enough, sickness! Enough, depression! God has said:

> *No weapon that is formed against thee shall prosper; and every tongue that shall rise against thee in judgment thou shalt condemn. This is the heritage of the servants of the LORD, and their righteousness is of me, saith the LORD.*
> Isaiah 54:17

If you will disallow a thing, then God will step in and change your situation.

Paul wrote to the Roman believers:

> *God forbid. How shall we, that are dead to sin, live any longer therein?*

Having Faith for New Things

For if we have been planted together in the likeness of his death, we shall be also in the likeness of his resurrection.

Now if we be dead with Christ, we believe that we shall also live with him: knowing that Christ being raised from the dead dieth no more; death hath no more dominion over him.

Romans 6:2, 5, and 8-9

There can be no more harassment from sin in the life of a believer and even from death. When Jesus was raised from the dead two thousand years ago, we were raised with Him. Death can no longer threaten us. We will sleep only when our assignment here on Earth is finished.

The devil knows this, but since our minds often don't, he uses what we don't know to imprison us. We are God's testimony. We are the proof that He is alive. Signs and wonders, new things, are our identity:

And they [the disciples], *when they had heard that he was alive, and had*

> *been seen of her* [Mary Magdalene], *believed not.*
>
> *After that he appeared in another form unto two of them, as they walked, and went into the country. And they went and told it unto the residue: neither believed they them.*
>
> *Afterward he appeared unto the eleven as they sat at meat, and upbraided them with their unbelief and hardness of heart, because they believed not them which had seen him after he was risen. And he said unto them, Go ye into all the world, and preach the gospel to every creature. He that believeth and is baptized shall be saved; but he that believeth not shall be damned. And these signs shall follow them that believe; In my name shall they cast out devils; they shall speak with new tongues.*
>
> Mark 16:11-17

Even these disciples *"believed not."* Therefore, you and I are being sent to act the part of Jesus. We must talk like Him, act like Him, and bear the same signs and wonders as He did. In order to do this, we must be convinced that we share the throne of grace with Him.

Yes, we have full access, and He told us to *"come boldly":*

> *Let us therefore come boldly unto the throne of grace, that we may obtain mercy, and find grace to help in time of need.* Hebrews 4:16

So, it's all up to you now. Don't be a coward! Step up and take your rightful place! Failure is not an option, for this Word is God speaking, not a man. Trapped within our spirit is the omnipotence of God to rule the Earth.

John wrote to the early Church:

> *These things have I written unto you that believe on the name of the Son of God; that ye may know that ye have eternal life, and that ye may believe on the name of the Son of God.*
> 1 John 5:13

Just believe, no matter what your physical senses are telling you. They can't see these promises, but in the Spirit, you can.

Our faith will take hold when we see the authority of the Word of God as if Christ Himself were standing before us physically, speaking to us. The Word of God does not *contain* life; it *is* life itself:

> *It is the spirit that quickeneth; the flesh profiteth nothing: the words that I speak unto you, they are spirit, and they are life.* John 6:63

We are not trying to believe, and we are not praying for faith; we are believers. We are in faith because we hear what our God says, and we know that He is the truth. So what are you trying to believe? We already have whatever He says we have:

> *Fear thou not; for I am with thee: be not dismayed; for I am thy God: I will strengthen thee; yea, I will help thee;*

yea, I will uphold thee with the right hand of my righteousness. Behold, all they that were incensed against thee shall be ashamed and confounded: they shall be as nothing; and they that strive with thee shall perish. Isaiah 41:10-11

Therefore let no man glory in men. For all things are yours; whether Paul, or Apollos, or Cephas, or the world, or life, or death, or things present, or things to come; all are yours; and ye are Christ's; and Christ is God's.
1 Corinthians 3:21-23

All too often we declare the faithfulness of Satan to do what he says he will do (steal, kill, and destroy), and through unbelief and fear, we declare God's inability to do what He has promised. He crowns the year with His goodness:

Thou crownest the year with thy goodness; and thy paths drop fatness.
Psalm 65:11

> *The angel of the LORD encampeth round about them that fear him, and delivereth them.* Psalm 34:7

> *And Jesus came and spake unto them, saying, All power is given unto me in Heaven and in earth. Go ye therefore, and teach all nations, baptizing them in the name of the Father, and of the Son, and of the Holy Ghost: teaching them to observe all things whatsoever I have commanded you: and, lo, I am with you alway, even unto the end of the world. Amen.* Matthew 28:18-20

You cannot be afraid of Satan and despise God and expect good results in your life. *"He that cometh to God must believe that he is"* (Hebrews 11:6), not just that He *was*. He *is*, and He is still doing wonders today, when we believe and trust Him even when what we are believing for doesn't seem to make sense.

God did not send the coronavirus; it's from the devil. You are of God, and therefore you cannot fear what God Himself has judged. Sickness of any sort is not for you. The psalmist boldly declared:

> *For he will rescue you from every trap*
> *and protect you from deadly disease.*
> *He will cover you with his feathers.*
> *He will shelter you with his wings.*
> *His faithful promises are your armor and protection.*
> *Do not be afraid of the terrors of the night,*
> *nor the arrow that flies in the day.*
> *Do not dread the disease that stalks in darkness,*
> *nor the disaster that strikes at midday.*
> *Though a thousand fall at your side,*
> *though ten thousand are dying around you,*
> *these evils will not touch you.*
> *Just open your eyes,*
> *and see how the wicked are punished.*
> *If you make the LORD your refuge,*
> *if you make the Most High your shelter,*
> *no evil will conquer you;*
> *no plague will come near your home.*

*For he will order his angels
to protect you wherever you go.
They will hold you up with their hands
so you won't even hurt your foot on a stone.
You will trample upon lions and cobras;
you will crush fierce lions and serpents
under your feet!
The Lord says, "I will rescue those who
love me.
I will protect those who trust in my
name.
When they call on me, I will answer;
I will be with them in trouble.
I will rescue and honor them.
I will reward them with a long life
and give them my salvation.*

Psalm 91:3-16, NLT

Now that you know your value, it's time to start rating yourself by Heaven's standard, not your own. Remember, you have been *"bought with a price"*:

Ye are bought with a price; be not ye the servants of men. 1 Corinthians 7:23

How much did God pay for you?

> *Forasmuch as ye know that ye were not redeemed with corruptible things, as silver and gold, from your vain conversation received by tradition from your fathers; but with the precious blood of Christ, as of a lamb without blemish and without spot.* 1 Peter 1:18-19

The world doesn't value you because they don't know your worth. Getting your information from people who don't know you is a sacrilege. They will confuse you and mold you to their own standards and ratings.

The attention of Heaven has been on you because Jesus Christ paid the price for you. Through this act, you and I become the most prized possessions of the Almighty. He said:

> *Since thou wast precious in my sight, thou hast been honourable, and I have loved thee: therefore will I give men for thee, and people for thy life.*
> Isaiah 43:4

The One that Heaven could not contain came down to reside within you and me. He is Emmanuel, God with us. See what the pagan Philistines had to say concerning Him:

> *And the Philistines were afraid, for they said, God is come into the camp. And they said, Woe unto us! for there hath not been such a thing heretofore. Woe unto us! who shall deliver us out of the hand of these mighty Gods? these are the Gods that smote the Egyptians with all the plagues in the wilderness.*
> 1 Samuel 4:7-8

Toward the end of Jesus' time on the Earth, He said:

> *I am with you always, even to the end of the age.* Matthew 28:20, NKJV

That's enough to strengthen any weakness. The report from God is that Jesus came to give you life, and this life cannot be quenched or stopped by darkness. Who has believed the report that slavery, oppression, poverty, and affliction has ended? (see Isaiah 53:1). The prophet Isaiah declared:

> *But he was wounded for our transgressions, he was bruised for our iniquities: the chastisement of our peace was upon him; and with his stripes we are healed.*
> Isaiah 53:5

It's all in past tense. *"The chastisement of our peace was upon him."* It's done. I have peace through Jesus Christ now, so I take peace now. Why should I wait? The Passion Translation renders this passage this way:

> *But it was because of our rebellious deeds that he was pierced and because of our sins that he was crushed. He endured the punishment that made us completely whole, and in his wounding we found our healing.*
> Isaiah 53:5, TPT

Yes, we found it, and we have it.

Understand the Power of Knowledge

Hosea wrote:

> *My people are destroyed for lack of knowledge: because thou hast rejected knowledge, I will also reject thee, that thou shalt be no priest to me: seeing thou hast forgotten the law of thy God, I will also forget thy children.* Hosea 4:6

Your victory begins with knowledge. It is what you know that announces your destiny. New things don't come to you just because you're a Christian. They come because you have the knowledge of the truth. When you're willing, God gives you insight into what is true and what is not.

Discovering the power of the Word (which is truth) makes you want to act on it. The Word is all God has for you to know. It tells you how God thinks about you, about His creative ability, and about what you are capable of doing in Christ.

Having Faith for New Things

When God said, *"Behold, I will do a new thing,"* He was not asking for you to have faith as a believer. He was asking for you to act. He not only creates things by His Word; He oversees others producing Word results:

> *Then said the L*ORD *unto me, Thou hast well seen: for I will hasten* [sleepless, watch] *my word to perform it.*
> Jeremiah 1:12

Doubting the Word is doubting God, the One who spoke it. He and His Word are one:

> *In the beginning was the Word, and the Word was with God, and the Word was God* John 1:1

That Word changed Mary's life, it changed Joseph's life, and it must change your life too. Agreement with God's Word releases heavenly favor into your life:

> *And Mary said, Behold the handmaid of the Lord; be it unto me according to thy word.* Luke 1:38

"Be it unto me according to thy word." Stop trying to explain your situation, and start acting on the Word. Too much of an explanation brings expiration. When you start acting on the Word, it simplifies your life and brings you to total victory.

Understand this: the Bible is God's revelation to man. It is what you can do that you have not yet attempted. It is the picture of the potential within you that you have not yet released. You can walk on water! You can turn a city around! God already approved that, but you have never yet attempted it. Why? Because you have never seen yourself doing it. But it's in you. That's why God said it. Remove the limitations, for God's Word is true.

Understand Divine connectivity.

This new being, called a new creation, or called a believer, was made in Heaven to manage the Earth:

> *The Father loveth the Son, and hath given all things into his hand.* John 3:35

> *I in them, and thou in me, that they may be made perfect in one; and that the world may know that thou hast sent me, and hast loved them, as thou hast loved me.* John 17:23

This new creation man was not created in dust, but rather in Christ.

> *For we are his workmanship, created in Christ Jesus unto good works, which God hath before ordained that we should walk in them.* Ephesians 2:10

This new creation man is a complicated being that not even the devil can understand or interpret. This new man is a *"partaker of the divine nature":*

> *Whereby are given unto us exceeding great and precious promises: that by these ye might be partakers of the divine nature, having escaped the corruption that is in the world through lust.*
> 2 Peter 1:4

Because this new creation man has the divine nature, he is connected to the throne room and is filled with the same Spirit that raised Jesus Christ from the dead. This makes him an oracle of God:

> *If any man speak, let him speak as the oracles of God; if any man minister, let him do it as of the ability which God giveth: that God in all things may be glorified Through Jesus Christ, to whom be praise and dominion for ever and ever. Amen.* 1 Peter 4:11

But until a believer knows himself, he will continue to live a life of slavery. He is capable of being fruitful in all things because he's attached to the Vine and is well nourished by that Vine. Jesus said:

> *I am the vine, ye are the branches: He that abideth in me, and I in him, the same bringeth forth much fruit: for without me ye can do nothing.* John 15:5

This new creation man is not subject to any devil. Why? Because his position has been changed, and everything that bows to the Lord Jesus also bows to him. He is now part of the Body of Christ:

> *Now ye are the body of Christ, and members in particular.*
> 1 Corinthians 12:27

This life of new things is based on divine connectivity. That means he now has the promise of Luke 10:19:

> *Behold, I give unto you power to tread on serpents and scorpions, and over all the power of the enemy: and nothing shall by any means hurt you.*

Sad to say, all too often this dynamic ability resident in every believer is trapped by religion, tradition, and human experience. The power is there, but it requires our cooperation to be released:

> *To whom God would make known what is the riches of the glory of this mystery among the Gentiles; which is Christ in you, the hope of glory: whom we preach, warning every man, and teaching every man in all wisdom; that we may present every man perfect in Christ Jesus: whereunto I also labour, striving according to his working, which worketh in me mightily.* Colossians 1:27-29

Christ is in you, and when He is in, you cannot be stopped by the Red Sea. Every obstacle must role away, just as the stone was rolled away from the entrance of Jesus' tomb.

That day His every accuser fell, and He is there with you and in you this very moment. May the trapped ability in you be loosed in and by the name of Jesus. The ability of God is released as that name is invoked:

> *And these signs shall follow them that believe; In my name shall they cast out devils; they shall speak with new tongues.* Mark 16:17

Having Faith for New Things

Here are some of the amazing promises awaiting the release of God's power in and through you:

> *Wherefore God also hath highly exalted him, and given him a name which is above every name: that at the name of Jesus every knee should bow, of things in heaven, and things in earth, and things under the earth; and that every tongue should confess that Jesus Christ is Lord, to the glory of God the Father.*
> Philippians 2:9-11

> *And whatsoever ye shall ask in my name, that will I do, that the Father may be glorified in the Son. If ye shall ask any thing in my name, I will do it.* John 14:13-14

Release the power now by declaring the Word of the living God, and get those new things in the days ahead. This year will be one of miracles and wonders everywhere you go in the name of Jesus Christ. The God in us wants to work miracles now:

For it is God which worketh in you both to will and to do of his good pleasure.
                    Philippians 2:13

Your connection with divinity is the foundation for new things happening in your life, and that is firmly established through Christ. That was Jesus' secret, and it can be yours too. He said:

I and my father are one.   John 10:30

He prayed for you and me:

Neither pray I for these alone, but for them also which shall believe on me through their word; that they all may be one; as thou, Father, art in me, and I in thee, that they also may be one in us: that the world may believe that thou hast sent me.   John 17:20-21

"That they also may be one in us." Based on that promise I decree today"

- I refuse to be devalued by any force or situation in the name of Jesus Christ.
- I decree by the Word of the living God that every limitation shall be removed now in the name of Jesus Christ.
- I am the Body of Christ. Therefore, no corruption is allowed here, no oppression, lack, or frustration in the name of Jesus Christ.

Amen!

Yes, when you have faith for new things, you can start *Ruling Your World.*

CHAPTER 3

RULING YOUR WORLD

Then God said, "Let Us (Father, Son, Holy Spirit) make man in Our image, according to Our likeness [not physical, but a spiritual personality and moral likeness]; and let them have complete authority over the fish of the sea, the birds of the air, the cattle, and over the entire earth, and over everything that creeps and crawls on the earth."

Genesis 1:26, AMP

When the purpose of a thing is not known, abuse is inevitable, and we lose its effectiveness. Prayer is not a religious thing; it's a God thing. It is a divine arrangement by which God has placed man in a position of authority and dominion. It is communicating and fellowshipping with God, the Creator, to bring to pass His purpose for creation. That's why the logical response to our prayers is an answer.

God created the heavens and the Earth, but He doesn't live here. He placed man here as the legal authority, and man must depend on God for ruling the Earth.

It is, therefore, illegal for God to operate here without human authority. Why? Because He designed it that way. He made the law and put Himself under it. It is prayer that makes God legal on the Earth:

> *Therefore he* [King Asa] *said to Judah, "Let us build these cities and make walls around them, and towers, gates, and bars, while the land is yet before us, because we have sought the LORD our God; we have sought Him, and He has given us rest on every side." So they built and prospered.* 2 Chronicles 14:7, NKJV

Jesus said to Peter:

> *And I also say to you that you are Peter, and on this rock I will build My church, and the gates of Hades shall not prevail against it. And I will give you the keys of the kingdom of heaven, and whatever you bind on earth will be bound in heaven, and whatever you loose on earth will be loosed in heaven."*
>
> Matthew 16:18-19, NKJV

This means that your prayer life determines your winning or losing. It's not in the hand of God. God remains faithful and will do His part, if and when you pray according to His rules. He is constant, but humans are the variable. Prayer was intended to be answered. When Jesus prayed at the tomb of Lazarus, He said:

> *"Father, I thank You that You have heard Me. And I know that You always hear Me, but because of the people who are standing by I said this, that they may believe that You sent Me."*
>
> John 11:41-42, NKJV

It should be the same with us:

> *So Jesus said to them again, "Peace to you! As the Father has sent Me, I also send you."* John 20:21, NKJV

Your access to the throne of grace is your covenant advantage and God-given privilege to rule your world:

> *Let us therefore come boldly to the throne of grace, that we may obtain mercy and find grace to help in time of need.* Hebrews 4:16, NKJV

Your colorful destiny is establish because of your link with Yahweh, the God of the whole Universe through the Abrahamic covenant:

> *And if you are Christ's, then you are Abraham's seed, and heirs according to the promise.* Galatians 3:29, NKJV

When you discover these truths and you take responsibility, you can recover all that you have lost and dominate life's circumstances. It's in your blood. You couldn't obtain these things on your own, but if you want them and you diligently hearken to the voice of the Lord your God, they will be yours.

Your announcement is already prepared, the set time for your manifestation is now. This is the time for the fulfilling of your God-given mandate on Earth:

> *"Thus says the LORD of hosts: 'In those days ten men from every language of the nations shall grasp the sleeve of a Jewish man, saying, "Let us go with you, for we have heard that God is with you."'"*
> Zechariah 8:23, NKJV

Why are so many believers not getting results in prayer and are frustrated as a result? It's because they don't pray according to God's rules. Here are some helpful tips on prayer:

1. Be specific in Your Prayer and Know What God's Word Says about the Matter

You would never go to a car dealership looking for tomatoes, and you would never go to Walmart looking for a yacht. You go to Walmart to get toothpaste, so you go right to the aisle that has a good variety of it, and you pick out the one you need. In the same way, you should never go to God without knowing what His Word says about what you're looking for.

That Word is the guarantee that what you want or need is available in God's store. Once you know it is, you can just go in and take it. The Word of God, therefore, is the foundation for answers to prayer, not your emotions or your tears. Go to God's Word first for your shopping, as if you are in a store. His Word is never out of date:

> *Heaven and earth will pass away, but My words will by no means pass away.* Matthew 24:35, NKJV

What God has promised is what God will do. Better said, what He has promised is what He has already done in Christ. The most important issue, therefore, in prayer is to get the Scriptures into your heart. Let the Word be a seed that is sown deep in your heart through meditation. Then, let your mouth speak it forth. Joshua declared:

> *This Book of the Law shall not depart from your mouth, but you shall meditate in it day and night, that you may observe to do according to all that is written in it. For then you will make your way prosperous, and then you will have good success.* Joshua 1:8, NKJV

You cannot doubt God when you know what His Word says about a given situation. If the Word says He has done it, then He has done it. No one can reverse that. If the Word says I am blessed, that's it. Nobody can make me poor. Why? Because the Word of God cannot fail. It speaks to the integrity of God Himself, and He simply will not deny Himself. He remains forever faithful.

Remember what God said about His Word:

> *Heaven and earth will pass away, but My words will by no means pass away.*
> Matthew 24:35, NKJV

Don't be terrified or feel terrible if you don't get immediate answers to your prayers. This is called *"the good fight of faith":*

> *Fight the good fight of faith, lay hold on eternal life, to which you were also called and have confessed the good confession in the presence of many witnesses.*
> 1 Timothy 6:12, NKJV

Remain faithful, and the resistance will eventually give up. Lay hold of the Word and refuse to let it go for any reason.

God doesn't play games. If what the Word has promised was not yours, it would never have been written. Now that it is written, it's yours. But you must put up a fight if you don't see it manifested.

Physically, if someone wants to take what is ours, we fight for it. For some reason, when it comes to the spiritual, we are much more passive. If you have paid for a house or a car, you will claim it as your rightful property. Well, Jesus paid for your health, your protection, and your prosperity. Fight for it by standing on the Word. It is your official receipt.

2. Ask God What You desire; Don't Just Assume

I find it very interesting that God want us to participate in our destiny and fulfillment in life by showing us how important we are in His presence. He said:

> *For your heavenly Father knows that you need all these things.*
> Matthew 6:32, NKJV

Wow! Even before we ask, He knows what we need. Nevertheless, He encourages us to ask. This is our privilege and responsibility:

And in that day you will ask Me nothing. Most assuredly, I say to you, whatever you ask the Father in My name He will give you. Until now you have asked nothing in My name. Ask, and you will receive, that your joy may be full. John 16:23-24, NKJV

Ask, and it will be given to you; seek, and you will find; knock, and it will be opened to you. For everyone who asks receives, and he who seeks finds, and to him who knocks it will be opened.
Matthew 7:7-8, NKJV

The amazing thing here is that you are in a class with God, and God believes that you have the ability to expect what you ask Him for:

Therefore I say to you, whatever things you ask when you pray, believe that you receive them, and you will have them.
Mark 11:24, NKJV

Ruling Your World

"You will have them!" This truth expressed here is so powerful. All that you will ever need is provided already, but in the realm of the Spirit, you must bring it to pass by your faith:

> *Blessed be the God and Father of our Lord Jesus Christ, who has blessed us with every spiritual blessing in the heavenly places in Christ.*
> Ephesians 1:3, NKJV

This was what Jesus saw when He fed the five thousand. The disciples were concerned that they were in a place where no food was available, the people were hungry, and it was getting late. Surely they should let the people go so that they could find food. Jesus just answered:

> *They do not need to go away. You give them something to eat.*
> Matthew 14:16, NKJV

When the disciples protested that they had so little food, only five small loaves and two fish, He said: *"Bring them here to Me"* (Matthew 14:18, NKJV). Then He told the multitudes to sit down and get ready to eat. He saw the food in the spirit realm. There was a need, and He knew the Father's love, so there was no question. They would be fed.

When He told Peter to go catch a fish with a coin in its mouth to pay the taxes for them both, Peter must have wondered. But, sure enough, the coin was there, and the taxes were paid:

> *Notwithstanding, lest we should offend them, go thou to the sea, and cast an hook, and take up the fish that first cometh up; and when thou hast opened his mouth, thou shalt find a piece of money: that take, and give unto them for me and thee.* Matthew 17:27

What the Word of God says is incontestable and never failing. That's why we, just as Father Abraham, can call things that are not as though they were:

> *(As it is written, I have made thee a father of many nations,) before him whom he believed, even God, who quickeneth the dead, and calleth those things which be not as though they were.*
>
> Romans 4:17

Don't act on your senses. They will fail you. *"Let the weak say, I am strong"* (Joel 3:10). That is believing faith.

3. Guard Your Mind

The center of enemy attack is not your body; it's your mind. The enemy will do anything under Heaven to convince you that you cannot get what you have asked for. He will say you are not qualified, but Jesus qualified you:

> *For Christ also hath once suffered for sins, the just for the unjust, that he might bring us to God, being put to death in the flesh, but quickened by the Spirit.* 1 Peter 3:18

I, even I, am he that blotteth out thy transgressions for mine own sake, and will not remember thy sins.
Isaiah 43:25

You have the services of the Advocate. He will stand for you and declare you justified. Stop thinking any thoughts that are not from God. Get your attention off of yourself and your limitations and onto the answer. See, or picture, the answer in your mind. Resist thoughts of doubt:

Be sober, be vigilant; because your adversary the devil, as a roaring lion, walketh about, seeking whom he may devour: whom resist stedfast in the faith, knowing that the same afflictions are accomplished in your brethren that are in the world. 1 Peter 5:8-9

Second Corinthians 10:3-5 teaches us to cast down carnal imaginations:

For though we walk in the flesh, we do not war after the flesh: (for the weapons of our warfare are not carnal, but mighty through God to the pulling down of strong holds;) casting down imaginations, and every high thing that exalteth itself against the knowledge of God, and bringing into captivity every thought to the obedience of Christ.

Cast down all thoughts, feelings, or even dreams that contradict the Word of God. They must die. Deal with them forcefully and decisively. You have the authority and ability to do that. Take this very seriously. If there is anything you must stop it's those wrong thoughts that come to your mind. However they come and from wherever, refuse to entertain them. The best way to avoid such thoughts is to fill your mind with good things:

Finally, brethren, whatsoever things are true, whatsoever things are honest, whatsoever things are just, whatsoever things are pure, whatsoever things are lovely, whatsoever things are of good report; if

there be any virtue, and if there be any praise, think on these things.
$\qquad$ Philippians 4:8

4. SEE YOURSELF IN YOUR PROMISE LAND

God's Word is given to create a picture of the future in our mind. When those pictures are created, the answers is already there. The challenge for many has been: How do I create a picture of my future? The answer is: You create the picture by meditating on the Word of God. When those pictures are there, faith is born:

> *This book of the law shall not depart out of thy mouth; but thou shalt meditate therein day and night, that thou mayest observe to do according to all that is written therein: for then thou shalt make thy way prosperous, and then thou shalt have good success.* Joshua 1:8

In this way, you can see your answers:

My son, attend to my words; incline thine ear unto my sayings. Let them not depart from thine eyes; keep them in the midst of thine heart. For they are life unto those that find them, and health to all their flesh. Proverbs 4:20-22. KJV

If the Word abides in you, you can't miss. Abraham knocked out barrenness and poverty by seeing himself in the purposes of God:

(As it is written, I have made thee a father of many nations,) before him whom he believed, even God, who quickeneth the dead, and calleth those things which be not as though they were. Who against hope believed in hope, that he might become the father of many nations, according to that which was spoken, So shall thy seed be. And being not weak in faith, he considered not his own body now dead, when he was about an hundred years old, neither yet the deadness of Sarah's womb: he staggered not at

the promise of God through unbelief; but was strong in faith, giving glory to God; and being fully persuaded that, what he had promised, he was able also to perform. Romans 4:17-21

You can do the same.

5. EXPRESS YOUR FAITH IN THANKSGIVING

Be careful for nothing; but in every thing by prayer and supplication with thanksgiving let your requests be made known unto God. Philippians 4:6

Your praise will remind God of His promises, not your problems. We are not intended to be telling God the same thing over and over again. He is fully aware of our circumstances, and He heard you the first time:

And this is the confidence that we have in him, that, if we ask any thing according to his will, he heareth us: and if we know

> *that he hear us, whatsoever we ask, we know that we have the petitions that we desired of him.* 1 John 5:14-15

Thank God because He is faithful. Your praise is the highest form of faith. Abraham was giving glory to God, even when the requests he was making had not yet materialized. Like him, we can pray, "I am persuaded that You have done it, so I give You praise in advance. Because Your Word says it, I take it. You are too faithful to lie. Thank You because favor is here for me. It is nothing I have done, but because I am the righteousness of God in Christ Jesus.

One of the most important things a person called to preach and teach the Word of God can do is to straighten out their thinking so that they stop sinking and stinking in life. We are to be the beauty and the glory of the King here on Earth:

> *Even every one that is called by my name: for I have created him for my glory, I have formed him; yea, I have made him.* Isaiah 43:7

The intention of God was not to have religion, creeds, or doctrines. His intention was to build the Kingdom of Heaven here on Earth. His desire was to have a nation of people doing His will and enjoying His blessings:

> *And ye shall be unto me a Kingdom of priests, and an holy nation. These are the words which thou shalt speak unto the children of Israel.* Exodus 19:6

> *That your days may be multiplied, and the days of your children, in the land which the LORD sware unto your fathers to give them, as the days of Heaven upon the earth.* Deuteronomy 11:21

Jesus said it this way:

> *After this manner therefore pray ye: Our Father which art in heaven, Hallowed be thy name. Thy kingdom come, Thy will be done in earth, as it is in heaven.*
> Matthew 6:9-10

Our stay on Earth is to be a replica of where God lives—void of sickness and all other forms of oppression. His intention was to set up a Kingdom that man would manage with all the power and influence of Heaven (see Genesis 1:26).

This world was to be our King's domain, with the authority of God, the power of God, the jurisdiction of God, the anointing of God, the government of God on Earth. This is why God told Adam and Eve that they wouldn't have to do anything. The King was to bring them all the provisions they needed:

> *And the LORD God commanded the man, saying, "Of every tree of the garden you may freely eat."* Genesis 2:16, NKJV

With this government, all that was required was obedience. As Jesus said, our heavenly Father knows what we need before we ask:

> *For your heavenly Father knows that you need all these things.*
> Matthew 6:32, NKJV

Ruling Your World

> *I sent you to reap that for which you have not labored; others have labored, and you have entered into their labors.*
> John 4:38, NKJV

Struggle and labor came with the Babylonian system, when man decided to get things for himself independent of God and His Kingdom. But God was King over the territory, and man was under His rule. The moment you were in the Kingdom (represented by the garden of Eden), you had control over the entire planet:

> *The LORD God planted a garden eastward in Eden, and there He put the man whom He had formed.*
> *Then the LORD God took the man and put him in the garden of Eden to tend and keep it.* Genesis 2:8 and 15, NKJV

God created the heavens and the Earth, but He planted the garden. The Earth was created, but the garden was planted. It was designed to receive input from God into the

Earth. That which was created was to support that which was planted.

Adam could have used what was created to make more gardens. Nothing worked against him as long as he aligned himself with the constitution of the King. This was total non-stress living.

The tree of knowledge of good and evil was there, but it could not hurt them, unless they disobeyed and ate from it. The King provided the constitution of the Kingdom for all the citizens to enjoy Heaven on Earth. This had nothing to do with religion at all; it was a lifestyle.

When man sinned, the first thing God did was to expel him from the Kingdom. Why? Because he was polluting the operation of the Kingdom. God now placed angels at the gates with flaming swords in their hands:

> *So He drove out the man; and He placed cherubim at the east of the garden of Eden, and a flaming sword which turned every way, to guard the way to the tree of life.* **Genesis 3:24, NKJV**

Religion came about because human beings wanted to get back into the Kingdom and didn't know how. They decided on something that made them feel they had done their best. Religion is man's activity or effort to reach out to God; the Kingdom is God's effort to reach out to man. Man's feeble efforts are in vain:

> *For by grace you have been saved through faith, and that not of yourselves; it is the gift of God, not of works, lest anyone should boast.* Ephesians 2:8-9, NKJV

Man's biggest problem now was that he didn't trust that God would still be loving toward him after what he had done. He was afraid that God would hurt him. He had lost confidence in God because of the lies the enemy had told him:

> *So he said, "I heard Your voice in the garden, and I was afraid because I was naked; and I hid myself."*
> Genesis 3:10, NKJV

God responded:

> *Who told you that you were naked? Have you eaten from the tree of which I commanded you that you should not eat?* Genesis 3:11, NKJV

Adam had lost his position in the Kingdom.

When Jesus came to Earth, His number one priority was to bring humanity back into the Kingdom (the garden). He told all those who would listen:

> *Repent, for the kingdom of heaven is at hand.* Matthew 4:17, NKJV

The Kingdom was here again, and man could go back into the garden and enjoy Kingdom living once again:

> *For after all these things the Gentiles seek. For your heavenly Father knows that you need all these things. But seek first the kingdom of God and His*

righteousness, and all these things shall be added to you.
Matthew 6:32-33, NKJV

You don't have to sweat to live. Living by the sweat of your brow was part of being under the curse. Jesus said to all, "Come and seek the Kingdom. All that you are looking for is provided there." Jesus is our Garden of Eden. He said, "In Me, you have peace":

Peace I leave with you, my peace I give unto you: not as the world giveth, give I unto you. Let not your heart be troubled, neither let it be afraid. John 14:27

These things I have spoken unto you, that in me ye might have peace. In the world ye shall have tribulation: but be of good cheer; I have overcome the world.
John 16:33

Religious people don't like these truths. They make all their efforts seem worthless (as they are). Never forget that there is a constitution that governs the Kingdom, and anyone who fails to recognize it will be left outside. As a believer in Jesus and citizen of His Kingdom, you can't do just whatever you feel like doing. All who are in the Kingdom must abide by the Word of the King. His Word is the law that governs the Kingdom. In order to enjoy the best of this Kingdom, you have to get onboard the program.

Jesus said it this way:

> *Come to Me, all you who labor and are heavy laden, and I will give you rest. Take My yoke upon you and learn from Me, for I am gentle and lowly in heart, and you will find rest for your souls.*
> Matthew 11:28-29, NKJV

The greatest search of mankind is not for money; it's for a way into God's Kingdom. It's not for health and soundness; it's for the Kingdom. Why? Because in the Kingdom, there is provision for every problem of every citizen. In the Kingdom, the glory of the King is seen in the life of His citizens.

Jesus commanded His disciples:

> *And heal the sick there, and say to them, "The kingdom of God has come near to you."* Luke 10:9, NKJV

> *Then He called His twelve disciples together and gave them power and authority over all demons, and to cure diseases.*
> *But when the multitudes knew it, they followed Him; and He received them and spoke to them about the kingdom of God, and healed those who had need of healing.* Luke 9:1 and 11, NKJV

It is impossible to understand the Kingdom and not seek it with all of your heart. Here's what Jesus said:

> *Again, the kingdom of heaven is like a merchant seeking beautiful pearls, who, when he had found one pearl of great price, went and sold all that he had and bought it.* Matthew 13:45-46, NKJV

Once you have found the Kingdom, it will provide for everything you need in life, and

Jesus came to bring us into this Kingdom reality:

> *He has delivered us from the power of darkness and conveyed us into the kingdom of the Son of His love.*
> Colossians 1:13, NKJV

Come into the Kingdom and see miracles manifested in your life.

The Kingdom of God is joy, peace, and righteousness in the Holy Ghost:

> *For the kingdom of God is not eating and drinking, but righteousness and peace and joy in the Holy Spirit.*
> Romans 13:17, NKJV

Wherever the Kingdom is preached, people rush in, happy that the answer is here at last.

The Kingdom is a system that you locate by the Word of the King, and once you have located it, you just enjoy its blessing. We can have it now, for the King has said that our labors can end now. This is so easy and simple that a child can understand and do it:

> *Then Jesus called for the children and said to the disciples, "Let the children come to me. Don't stop them! For the Kingdom of God belongs to those who are like these children. I tell you the truth, anyone who doesn't receive the Kingdom of God like a child will never enter it."* Luke 18:16-17, NLT

Children believe everything they're told. They don't have time for unforgiveness. They are confident of their parents and dependent upon them. They are not ashamed or intimidated. Come as little children. The table is set, and the King has spoken. *"Believe that you receive"* today:

> *Therefore I say to you, whatever things you ask when you pray, believe that you receive them, and you will have them.*
> Mark 11:24, NKJV

It doesn't matter what others are saying. It's all in the heavenly Constitution. If it's not true, then the Scriptures are lies, and the God of the whole Universe cannot lie. We don't pray just because we have to; we must believe and that's it. God will always make His Word good.

Never forget, you didn't bring yourself into the Kingdom; Jesus did it, and you don't have to press Him to fulfill His Word. His Word is already settled. Believe Him and thank Him now for your healing. If the Word says it, God will make it good. Just believe, and leave the performance of it to Him:

> *Blessed is she who believed, for there will be a fulfillment of those things which were told her from the Lord.*
> Luke 1:45, NKJV

The reason many don't see the glory of the Kingdom is because the Administrator has been neglected. Who is He? He is the Holy Spirit:

And I will ask the Father, and He will give you another Comforter (Counselor, Helper, Intercessor, Advocate, Strengthener, and Standby), that He may remain with you forever.
John 14:16, AMPC

Declare with me now:

- Father, in the name of Jesus Christ, I am in the Kingdom. I take my healing and deliverance now in Jesus' name.
- I paralyze all efforts to stop my joy and peace this day in the name of Jesus Christ.
- I walk in abundant favor and peace, for I am in the Kingdom now in Jesus' name.
- Father, in the name of Jesus Christ, I receive the baptism of fresh fire.

Amen!

Yes, it's time to start *Ruling Your World!*

Chapter 4

Discovering Covenant Access

And God blessed them, and God said unto them, Be fruitful, and multiply, and replenish the earth, and subdue it: and have dominion over the fish of the sea, and over the fowl of the air, and over every living thing that moveth upon the earth. Genesis 1:28

The instructions found in the Scriptures hold the keys to life and come with the ability to perform the task. God said we are to *"be fruitful."*

That was all Adam needed, for every material and every ability required was supplied, to make the Word of the Lord good. Whatever will make you an outstanding accomplisher, receive it now in Jesus' name.

People and environments have told us so many lies that we now find it difficult to believe the truths of the Scriptures. If God said we are to be fruitful, then we can and must be fruitful.

"Be fruitful" is a divine pronouncement that God made over His creation, and it was the first word that manifested the blessing of God over man. *"Be fruitful!"*

It was out of being fruitful that we were to multiply and replenish the Earth. This was not your wish; it was a divine agenda. God wants you to be fruitful, and since the Word of the Lord cannot go unfulfilled, your fruitfulness starts today:

> *And the LORD shall make thee plenteous in goods, in the fruit of thy body, and in the fruit of thy cattle, and in the fruit of thy ground, in the land which the LORD sware unto thy fathers to give thee.*
> Deuteronomy 28:11

Never forget, by covenant you must be fruitful. You were redeemed to be fruitful:

> *Christ hath redeemed us from the curse of the law, being made a curse for us: for it is written, Cursed is every one that hangeth on a tree: that the blessing of Abraham might come on the Gentiles through Jesus Christ; that we might receive the promise of the Spirit through faith.*
>
> *Wherefore then serveth the law? It was added because of transgressions, till the seed should come to whom the promise was made; and it was ordained by angels in the hand of a mediator.*
>
> Galatians 3:13-14 and 19

You are commanded to be fruitful, and you are ordained to be fruitful:

> *Ye have not chosen me, but I have chosen you, and ordained you, that ye should go and bring forth fruit, and that your fruit should remain: that whatsoever ye*

shall ask of the Father in my name, he may give it you. John 15:16

Lo, children are an heritage of the Lord: and the fruit of the womb is his reward. Psalm 127:3

To be fruitful is to be creative and produce, and it's to fill the Earth with results. It is to demonstrate God's great love for His children.

There are four major areas of fruitfulness spoken of here that make life fulfilling. You must be resolute in your heart to get all of them, but they are fully paid for.

1. Spiritual Fruitfulness

If you are not fruitful spiritually, you are vulnerable. You are prey for the enemy. To be spiritually barren is death and frustration, blind to every plan of God for your life:

And beside this, giving all diligence, add to your faith virtue; and to virtue knowledge; and to knowledge temperance; and

> *to temperance patience; and to patience godliness; and to godliness brotherly kindness; and to brotherly kindness charity. For if these things be in you, and abound, they make you that ye shall neither be barren nor unfruitful in the knowledge of our Lord Jesus Christ. But he that lacketh these things is blind, and cannot see afar off, and hath forgotten that he was purged from his old sins.*
> 2 Peter 1:5-9

> *For bodily exercise profiteth little: but godliness is profitable unto all things, having promise of the life that now is, and of that which is to come.* 1 Timothy 4:8

Spiritual barrenness destroyed the golden destiny of Esau. In his ignorance, he wondered what, if anything, his birthright would do for him:

> *Lest there be any fornicator, or profane person, as Esau, who for one morsel of meat sold his birthright. For ye know*

how that afterward, when he would have inherited the blessing, he was rejected: for he found no place of repentance, though he sought it carefully with tears.
Hebrews 12:16-17

Spiritual blindness will waste your years and limit your progress. Jacob said:

*Surely the L*ORD *is in this place, and I knew it not.* Genesis 28:16

He wasted twenty years of toil before he discovered this. If you are not developing your spiritual capacity, you will not be fruitful.

Fruitfulness is measurable. Fruitfulness in soul winning. Fruitfulness is having the fruit of the Spirit in your life, in your service to God, and in your commitment to His Kingdom.

David said:

*I was glad when they said unto me, Let us go into the house of the L*ORD*.*
Psalm 122:1

This was David's delight, and the result was that he was fruitful. I decree now that your spirit be opened for an outpouring of the Spirit of God upon your life in Jesus' name.

Spiritual fruitfulness will prevent the enemy from taking advantage of you. You and I are living and walking in the midst of serpents and scorpions. Spiritual fruitfulness will put you in charge.

But this is not automatic. You must make yourself available for it. Just because you are enrolled in school and pay tuition doesn't mean that you can pass the exams. You must make an effort to attend classes, learn the material, and take and pass the exams. Why are you running from training in the things of the Spirit? The enemy hates you. Take him out now and find spiritual fruitfulness.

2. Fruitfulness of the Body

God has not destined us to be barren. Again, fruit is our reward:

> *Lo, children are an heritage of the Lord: and the fruit of the womb is his reward.* Psalm 127:3

Whatever holds your womb in bondage be loosed now in Jesus' name. Today we limit childbearing through doctors' prescriptions. Thank God for that, but God gives us children. He is the manufacturer of them. He cannot deny the happiness of His kids:

> *Know ye that the LORD he is God: it is he that hath made us, and not we ourselves; we are his people, and the sheep of his pasture.* Psalm 100:3

For all those who are believing God for the fruit of the womb, I now speak. By the authority in the name of Jesus, I command your womb to be opened:

> *And the LORD visited Sarah as he had said, and the LORD did unto Sarah as he had spoken. For Sarah conceived, and bare Abraham a son in his old age, at*

> *the set time of which God had spoken to him.* Genesis 21:1-2

In the days ahead, the Lord will also remember you. His promise is:

> *He maketh the barren woman to keep house, and to be a joyful mother of children. Praise ye the LORD.* Psalm 113:9

3. FRUITFULNESS OF THE LAND

For your land to be fruitful means for you to prosper in everything you do. The land where you dwell is an asset to you. That land must not eat you up:

> *And they brought up an evil report of the land which they had searched unto the children of Israel, saying, The land, through which we have gone to search it, is a land that eateth up the inhabitants thereof; and all the people that we saw in it are men of a great stature.*
> Numbers 13:32

Whatever has attempted to eat up your efforts, I curse now in Jesus' name. I decree to the land. Whatever of mine you have swallowed, vomit it up now in Jesus' name.

Can the Earth hear? Yes, it can:

> *O earth, earth, earth, hear the word of the LORD.* Jeremiah 22:29

Your land was designed to produce results. Whatever you put into the ground should grow. Even if you don't plant, the land is given to help you. When you cannot prosper on the land, that is called barrenness, and you are not to be barren in any way:

> *Then Isaac sowed in that land, and received in the same year an hundredfold: and the Lord blessed him. And the man waxed great, and went forward, and grew until he became very great: for he had possession of flocks, and possession of herds, and great store of servants: and the Philistines envied him.*
> Genesis 26:12-14

Did God love Isaac more than He loves you? Absolutely not. Your land should prosper too.

4. Fruitfulness for Your Cattle

This speaks of your business. Everything you touch should turn to gold:

> *And the LORD shall make thee plenteous in goods, in the fruit of thy body, and in the fruit of thy cattle, and in the fruit of thy ground, in the land which the LORD sware unto thy fathers to give thee.*
> Deuteronomy 28:11

Some are not able to give testimony to great results in their life. Prosperity starts for you now in Jesus' name. That is a command.

God said:

> *And he shall be like a tree planted by the rivers of water, that bringeth forth his fruit in his season; his leaf also shall not*

> *wither; and whatsoever he doeth shall prosper.* Psalm 1:3

> *Therefore God give thee of the dew of heaven, and the fatness of the earth, and plenty of corn and wine: let people serve thee, and nations bow down to thee: be lord over thy brethren, and let thy mother's sons bow down to thee: cursed be every one that curseth thee, and blessed be he that blesseth thee.*
> Genesis 27:28-29

The blessing of God is beyond the economy of any nation. Those who believe look to Him, their faces are lightened, and they are not ashamed:

> *They looked unto him, and were lightened: and their faces were not ashamed.* Psalm 34:5

Claim that promise as your own today.

Understand that It Is Your Right to Be Fruitful

Genesis 1:28 is your birthright. The manifestation of God's blessing is fruitfulness. All of Hell knows this and all of the Universe knows it, and they must obey. First, however, you must know that this promise is yours:

> *He shall cause them that come of Jacob to take root: Israel shall blossom and bud, and fill the face of the world with fruit.* Isaiah 27:6

Claim it today!

Know that Fruitfulness Is a Reward for Serving God

Serving God comes with a reward. You simply cannot serve Him in vain:

> *And ye shall serve the LORD your God, and he shall bless thy bread, and thy*

water; and I will take sickness away from the midst of thee. There shall nothing cast their young, nor be barren, in thy land: the number of thy days I will fulfil. Exodus 23:25-26

Consider the fruitfulness of King Uzziah:

And he sought God in the days of Zechariah, who had understanding in the visions of God: and as long as he sought the Lord, God made him to prosper. And he went forth and warred against the Philistines, and brake down the wall of Gath, and the wall of Jabneh, and the wall of Ashdod, and built cities about Ashdod, and among the Philistines. And God helped him against the Philistines, and against the Arabians that dwelt in Gurbaal, and the Mehunims.

And the Ammonites gave gifts to Uzziah: and his name spread abroad even to the entering in of Egypt; for he strengthened himself exceedingly.

> *Moreover Uzziah built towers in Jerusalem at the corner gate, and at the valley gate, and at the turning of the wall, and fortified them. Also he built towers in the desert, and digged many wells: for he had much cattle, both in the low country, and in the plains: husbandmen also, and vine dressers in the mountains, and in Carmel: for he loved husbandry.* 2 Chronicles 26:5-10

The same promise of fruitfulness is yours:

> *These things dominate the thoughts of unbelievers, but your heavenly Father already knows all your needs. Seek the Kingdom of God above all else, and live righteously, and he will give you everything you need.*
> Matthew 6:32-33, NLT

MAKE THE WORD OF GOD, WITH ITS PROMISE OF FRUITFULNESS, A PRIORITY IN YOUR LIFE, NO MATTER THE CIRCUMSTANCES

Discovering Covenant Access

The major goal of the enemy is to make you feel that the Word of God has failed you. You must make the decision to live your life as if there is no other option than what God says. If what you believe is not attacked by the enemy, then you're not believing God's promises yet.

The enemy causes what appears to be a contradiction of faith. Things seem to be going against what the Word of God says. What are we to do when this happens? We must stir ourselves and forcefully declare the Word of God in faith, standing on His unfailing promises.

When God told Abraham He was going to bless him and make him fruitful, almost immediately there was famine in the land, and a pagan king took his wife. Abraham was already old, and it suddenly seemed that there was no hope. The enemy wants to frustrate you too. What did Abraham do?

And Abraham's faith did not weaken, even though, at about 100 years of age, he figured his body was as good

> *as dead—and so was Sarah's womb. Abraham never wavered in believing God's promise. In fact, his faith grew stronger, and in this he brought glory to God. He was fully convinced that God is able to do whatever he promises.*
>
> Romans 4:19-21, NLT

Make your stand for truth too.

MAKE A CHOICE TO BE FRUITFUL

When you know that fruitfulness is the will of God, then make a choice for it. God doesn't make choices for us. He shows us what is available by His Word, and we have to make the choices:

> *Today I have given you the choice between life and death, between blessings and curses. Now I call on heaven and earth to witness the choice you make. Oh, that you would choose life, so that you and your descendants might live!*
>
> Deuteronomy 30:19, NLT

Make your choice to be fruitful and then stand by it.

Again, it's interesting to know that the first blessing God gave to man was the blessing of fruitfulness. This was much more than just bearing children. Let's look at Genesis 1:28 again:

> *Then God blessed them and said, "Be fruitful and multiply. Fill the earth and govern it. Reign over the fish in the sea, the birds in the sky, and all the animals that scurry along the ground."* (NLT)

This word *fruitful* is from the Hebrew word *p'ru*. It means "to bear fruits, bring forth,to grow and to increase." Fruitfulness is not an accident and doesn't happen by chance. It is only the intervention of the Almighty that brings about fruitfulness:

> *Acknowledge that the LORD is God!*
> *He made us, and we are his.*
> *We are his people, the sheep of his pasture.* Psalm 100:3, NLT

Ruling Your World

God has an agenda to establish your fruitfulness, and your fruit bearing can even continue into old age. God said to Abraham, *"I will make you extremely fruitful"*:

> *I will make you extremely fruitful. Your descendants will become many nations, and kings will be among them!*
> Genesis 17:6, NLT

Fruitfulness terminates dryness and brings an end to drought and shame. It breaks the barriers of every barrenness. We are then able to produce results beyond human strength. Why? Because God is for us and with us. We are breaking all barriers and getting results in unusual places. It must happen, for God is true:

> *For the word of God will never fail.*
> Luke 1:37, NLT

With God on our side, nothing is impossible to us. We will bring forth much fruit in the name of Jesus Christ and for His glory.

Discovering Covenant Access

Let's come to this understanding: the same force that created the Universe and called it *"very good"* pronounced our fruitfulness. It was not just someone's advice or our own wish. It is a command of God.

He spoke, "Light be! Sun be!" and they were. Then He said, "Be fruitful!" Now everything in your life must adjust to that divine command. The voice of the Lord is full of majesty. The voice of the Lord is powerful. It cannot be resisted. Every resistance to your fruitfulness is cursed this day in the name of Jesus Christ.

Fruitfulness was not just the wish or dream of Adam or Eve; it was a divine agenda. Adam and Eve didn't do it; God did. He created man, already packaged to bring forth. There is a seed in you that is capable of producing a harvest, a fruitfulness—in your body, in your finances, and in your marriage:

> *They are like trees planted along the riverbank,*
>   *bearing fruit each season.*

> *Their leaves never wither,*
> *and they prosper in all they do.*
> Psalm 1:3, NLT

It is, therefore, important that we know and understand that fruitfulness works through the keys of the Kingdom. When these keys are used, uncommon results are the natural response.

1. The Foundation For Fruitfulness Is Knowing That God Is In You!

Yes, that is what makes you extraordinary. All the extraordinary feats that Jesus did when He was on Earth were based on God the Father being with Him and in Him:

> *For through him God created everything*
> *in the heavenly realms and on earth.*
> *He made the things we can see*
> *and the things we can't see —*
> *such as thrones, kingdoms, rulers, and*
> *authorities in the unseen world.*

Everything was created through him and for him.
He existed before anything else,
  and he holds all creation together.
Christ is also the head of the church,
  which is his body.
He is the beginning,
  supreme over all who rise from the dead.
  So he is first in everything.
For God in all his fullness
  was pleased to live in Christ,
Colossians 1:16-19, NLT

For God wanted them to know that the riches and glory of Christ are for you Gentiles, too. And this is the secret: Christ lives in you. This gives you assurance of sharing his glory.
Colossians 1:27, NLT

For in Christ lives all the fullness of God in a human body. So you also are complete through your union with Christ, who is the head over every ruler and authority.   Colossians 2:9-10, NLT

Ruling Your World

The life that has been imparted to you is key to experiencing uncommon results. That was the life that entered the dust, and that dust became a living soul:

> *And the Lord God formed man of the dust of the ground, and breathed into his nostrils the breath of life; and man became a living soul.* Genesis 2:7

That life entered into Peter, and he became a rock:

> *And I say also unto thee, That thou art Peter, and upon this rock I will build my church; and the gates of hell shall not prevail against it. And I will give unto thee the keys of the kingdom of heaven: and whatsoever thou shalt bind on earth shall be bound in heaven: and whatsoever thou shalt loose on earth shall be loosed in heaven.* Matthew 16:18-19

It's your turn now. God is with you and in you. Go forth and do exploits.

2. You Need Your Seed in the Right Environment for Fruitfulness to Happen

Yes, you need the right environment for your seed. Until you have seed mentality, you can't experience a total harvest. You are a seed, and God planted you here on Earth:

To all who mourn in Israel,
  he will give a crown of beauty for ashes,
a joyous blessing instead of mourning,
  festive praise instead of despair.
In their righteousness, they will be like great oaks
  that the LORD has planted for his own glory. Isaiah 61:3, NLT

Your destiny is a seed, and we believers are called *"the seed of Abraham"* (2 Corinthians 11:22). How much a seed produces depends on the place where it is planted. When you are around people who don't inspire you, you will expire. Carefully select your environment. Your seed (your vision) is powerful, but a toxic environment can kill it.

Would we have ever heard of Peter if he had not been around Jesus? King Saul was called a prophet because he was with the prophets (see 1 Samuel 10:11). The anointing where you are falls on you. Don't be afraid to be isolated, and when you are around other people, relate with people who challenge you, not people who indulge you. Go to places where you are celebrated, not just tolerated.

The rod of Aaron budded because it was placed in the Holy of Holies. Your destiny is bound to be fruitful if you are found in God's presence:

> *Blessed is the man that walketh not in the counsel of the ungodly, nor standeth in the way of sinners, nor sitteth in the seat of the scornful. But his delight is in the law of the LORD; and in his law doth he meditate day and night.* Psalm 1:1-2

> *The LORD hear thee in the day of trouble; the name of the God of Jacob defend thee;*

send thee help from the sanctuary, and strengthen thee out of Zion; remember all thy offerings, and accept thy burnt sacrifice; Selah. Psalm 20:1-3

Those that be planted in the house of the Lord shall flourish in the courts of our God. Psalm 92:13

3. Fellowship with the Holy Spirit Is Your Sunshine for Development

No seed grows without sunlight. The sun provides the energy plants need to convert carbon dioxide and water into carbohydrates and oxygen. That process is called photosynthesis.

If you are wondering why your efforts are not producing results, you may just need more sunlight. When the Holy Spirit breathes on you, He will produce results that will amaze you and everyone else.

No matter how bad your situation or the economy, your relationship with the Holy Spirit will change your level of productivity:

> *In the beginning God created the heaven and the earth. And the earth was without form, and void; and darkness was upon the face of the deep. And the Spirit of God moved upon the face of the waters. And God said, Let there be light: and there was light.* Genesis 1:1-3

Nothing came into manifestation until the Spirit moved, and it is the same today:

> *Upon the land of my people shall come up thorns and briers; yea, upon all the houses of joy in the joyous city: because the palaces shall be forsaken; the multitude of the city shall be left; the forts and towers shall be for dens for ever, a joy of wild asses, a pasture of flocks; until the spirit be poured upon us from on high, and the wilderness be a fruitful field, and the fruitful field be counted for a forest.* Isaiah 32:13-15

Discovering Covenant Access

When the Holy Spirit is with you, you can't run dry. That Spirit was poured out on believers after the resurrection and ascension of our Lord Jesus Christ:

> *Nevertheless I tell you the truth; It is expedient for you that I go away: for if I go not away, the Comforter will not come unto you; but if I depart, I will send him unto you.* John 16:7

> *And I will pray the Father, and he shall give you another Comforter, that he may abide with you for ever; even the Spirit of truth; whom the world cannot receive, because it seeth him not, neither knoweth him: but ye know him; for he dwelleth with you, and shall be in you.* John 14:16-17

The Spirit came for our benefit. Don't take Him for granted. Take time to fellowship with Him. Talk to Him. Ask Him questions. Thank Him. Worship Him. That's what fellowship is all about:

> *As they ministered to the Lord, and fasted, the Holy Ghost said, Separate me Barnabas and Saul for the work whereunto I have called them. And when they had fasted and prayed, and laid their hands on them, they sent them away.*
>
> Acts 13:2-3

The ultimate purpose of the Holy Spirit is to help enforce the Word of God and bring it to fruition in our lives:

> *Ye have not chosen me, but I have chosen you, and ordained you, that ye should go and bring forth fruit, and that your fruit should remain: that whatsoever ye shall ask of the Father in my name, he may give it you.* John 15:16

The Spirit is the Helper and the Messenger of the covenant. Fruitfulness that is beyond this world order can only be achieved by the force of the Spirit of God. It happened to Mary:

And the angel answered and said unto her, The Holy Ghost shall come upon thee, and the power of the Highest shall overshadow thee: therefore also that holy thing which shall be born of thee shall be called the Son of God. Luke 1:35

The Spirit also empowers you to bring forth. It was not Mary's prayer or vision that brought Jesus into the world; it was God's vision. But that vision was energized by the Spirit of God. Get plenty of sunshine.

4. Fertilize Yourself by Inspiring Yourself with Right Words and Protecting Your Spirit from Wrong Words

Words are very powerful, and they ultimately determine your results. Peter heard something that changed his life forever:

And Simon answering said unto him, Master, we have toiled all the night, and have taken nothing: nevertheless at thy word I will let down the net. Luke 5:5

The enemy has deceived people into thinking that words are nothing more than ordinary sounds. No, words contain spiritual force:

> *For verily I say unto you, That whosoever shall say unto this mountain, Be thou removed, and be thou cast into the sea; and shall not doubt in his heart, but shall believe that those things which he saith shall come to pass; he shall have whatsoever he saith.*
> Mark 11:23

The reason words are often not producing the desired result is that people don't believe in them. If you were crying about something, I could talk to you, and soon you would be dancing. Words are just that powerful. They can inspire us and cause us to get our desired results.

If you are depressed, condemned, feeling like a failure, and always saying "I can't," check what you are hearing. That is probably what's killing the seed in you.

Your destiny is so great that you simply must fertilize it with right words. The Bible says:

> *How forcible are right words! but what doth your arguing reprove?* Job 6:25

5. Consciously Connect with the Vine, and You Will Be Fruitful.

> *I am the vine, ye are the branches: He that abideth in me, and I in him, the same bringeth forth much fruit: for without me ye can do nothing.*
> John 15:5

If you would declare this daily and walk in the consciousness of it, you will be living a life of results.

- I decree, in agreement with God today, that I am fruitful in the name of Jesus Christ.
- I curse every dryness and limitation. Get out of my life now in Jesus' name!

- I receive grace to walk in wisdom and understanding.
- Holy Spirit, move over my life now in the name of Jesus. Create an unusual, uncommon result in Jesus' name.

Yes, when you discover covenant access, you can start *Ruling Your World!*

Chapter 5

Securing Your Future

Heaven and earth shall pass away, but my words shall not pass away.
                    Matthew 24:35

Until You accept the Scriptures as the truth from God, you cannot secure your future. The Scriptures are God's voice to our generation, and everything in the Universe is designed to obey the voice of God:

Mine hand also hath laid the foundation of the earth, and my right hand hath spanned the heavens: when I call unto them, they stand up together.
                    Isaiah 48:13

God's voice is full of majesty and strength. Everything was created by the Word:

> *All things were made by him; and without him was not any thing made that was made.* John 1:3

> *The Son radiates God's own glory and expresses the very character of God, and he sustains everything by the mighty power of his command. When he had cleansed us from our sins, he sat down in the place of honor at the right hand of the majestic God in heaven.*
> Hebrews 1:3, NLT

> *And Jesus said unto them, I am the bread of life: he that cometh to me shall never hunger; and he that believeth on me shall never thirst.* John 6:35

When we are careful to follow God's Word, His voice, total satisfaction is guaranteed. This work has to be done on the inside of you.

Securing Your Future

You did not come to Jesus on your own; God gave you to Jesus. It was not an accident. He searched for you and located you in the world, and then He gave you to Jesus on purpose:

> *My Father, which gave them me, is greater than all; and no man is able to pluck them out of my Father's hand.*
> John 10:29

> *All that the Father giveth me shall come to me; and him that cometh to me I will in no wise cast out.* John 6:37

This why Jesus could say that of all that the Father had given Him, He would lose none. The life that He gave to us is the proof that you can never be barren. That life carries all that is in God.

God has given us His very life:

> *In him was life; and the life was the light of men.* John 1:4

That light shattered darkness. With that light, no matter how much heat comes, you cannot be burned. No matter how much water comes, you cannot be drowned:

> *My sheep hear my voice, and I know them, and they follow me: and I give unto them eternal life; and they shall never perish, neither shall any man pluck them out of my hand. My Father, which gave them me, is greater than all; and no man is able to pluck them out of my Father's hand.* John 10:27-29

You cannot afford to rely on your feelings. Isaac depended on feelings and mistook Jacob for Esau. Don't worry about feeling it; just believe it. You have the life of God in you now.

Enforcing your fruitfulness is the ministry of the Holy Spirit and your understanding of your divine placement by redemption. You have authority here on Earth to dominate and become a god to every situation:

And the LORD said unto Moses, See, I have made thee a god to Pharaoh: and Aaron thy brother shall be thy prophet.
Exodus 7:1

Here are some tips on how to make that become a reality:

1. MEDITATE ON GOD'S WORD DAY AND NIGHT

Blessed is the man that walketh not in the counsel of the ungodly, nor standeth in the way of sinners, nor sitteth in the seat of the scornful. But his delight is in the law of the LORD; and in his law doth he meditate day and night. And he shall be like a tree planted by the rivers of water, that bringeth forth his fruit in his season; his leaf also shall not wither; and whatsoever he doeth shall prosper.
Psalm 1:1-3

Without meditation in the Word of God, you cannot possibly access what is in His heart.

Ruling Your World

Reading the Word will give you information, but meditation on it will give you understanding and revelation. When you have understanding, wisdom is then easy. You now know:

> *This book of the law shall not depart out of thy mouth; but thou shalt meditate therein day and night, that thou mayest observe to do according to all that is written therein: for then thou shalt make thy way prosperous, and then thou shalt have good success.* Joshua 1:8

It is your depth of understanding of God and His ways that will determine the level of your results and your fruitfulness. The same seed can be sown, but it may produce thirtyfold, sixtyfold, or one hundredfold. Based on what? Based on the understanding of the sower.

The Word of God is a spiritual seed, but you cannot profit from it if you don't understand it:

> *But he that received seed into the good ground is he that heareth the word, and*

> *understandeth it; which also beareth fruit, and bringeth forth, some an hundredfold, some sixty, some thirty.*
> Matthew 13:23

Your fruitfulness is by the aid of the Spirit of God through understanding. The issue, therefore, is not with God; it's with you. He has left us many promises and most of them were given before you ever came on the scene. He is ready to fulfill those promises, if and when you are ready to cooperate and agree with Him.

Meditation on the Word will change your carnal way of thinking:

> *And be not conformed to this world: but be ye transformed by the renewing of your mind, that ye may prove what is that good, and acceptable, and perfect, will of God.*
> Romans 12:2

If you walk with God, you will discover that the world is not really thinking at all. With the world, it's all guesses and hypotheses. Man says, "Unless God would open the windows of Heaven, this cannot happen." No wonder the Bible says that *"the foolishness of God is wiser than men"*:

> *Because the foolishness of God is wiser than men; and the weakness of God is stronger than men.*
> 1 Corinthians 1:25

> *For the wisdom of this world is foolishness with God. For it is written, He taketh the wise in their own craftiness.*
> 1 Corinthians 3:19

How could a simple touch stop the flow of blood that has going on for twelve years, after the woman in question had spent all her money on doctors and medicines? How could the muddy waters of the Jordan River wash away leprosy? This is all meaningless to man, but meditation on the Word of God will change your views about life and strengthen your faith in God.

2. Decree the Word of God over Your Life without Wavering

If you are not covenant minded, you will be frustrated in this evil world:

> *That ye may be blameless and harmless, the sons of God, without rebuke, in the midst of a crooked and perverse nation, among whom ye shine as lights in the world.* Philippians 2:15

> *Have respect unto the covenant: for the dark places of the earth are full of the habitations of cruelty.* Psalm 74:20. KJV

"God can be trusted to keep his promises":

> *Let us hold tightly without wavering to the hope we affirm, for God can be trusted to keep his promise.* Hebrews 10:23, NLT

Therefore, declare the Word with boldness. God's Word is His bond, His unfailing and never-changing covenant.

Your present captivity is not the end of the story. God has vowed to take you to a wealthy place, and it is sign of disobedience to live a life without results. God has armed you with authority to do what needs to be done. He said:

> *Thus says the LORD,*
> *The Holy One of Israel, and his Maker:*
> *"Ask Me of things to come concerning My sons;*
> *And concerning the work of My hands, you command Me.*
>
> Isaiah 45:11, NKJV

Jesus said that just as the Father sent Him, He (Jesus) is sending us:

> *So Jesus said to them again, "Peace to you! As the Father has sent Me, I also send you."* John 20:21, NKJV

Jesus saw the storms, but He was not moved by them. Instead, He commanded, *"Peace, be still!"* (Mark 4:39). Whatever is set against you today, I command it to be destroyed. How can I say that? Because with Christ in us, we have the same potential.

Jesus also said that we are *"joint heirs"* with Him:

> *The Spirit Himself bears witness with our spirit that we are children of God, and if children, then heirs—heirs of God and joint heirs with Christ, if indeed we suffer with Him, that we may also be glorified together.*
> Romans 8:16-17, NKJV

> *Most assuredly, I say to you, he who believes in Me, the works that I do he will do also; and greater works than these he will do, because I go to My Father.*
> John 14:12, NKJV

> *So the men marveled, saying, "Who can this be, that even the winds and the sea obey Him?"* Matthew 8:27, NKJV

Just as men marveled at what Jesus said and did, this is why you, too, have been sent.

Immediately he arose, took up the bed, and went out in the presence of them all, so that all were amazed and glorified God, saying, "We never saw anything like this!" Mark 2:12, NKJV

And they were all amazed, and they glorified God and were filled with fear, saying, "We have seen strange things today!" Luke 5:26, NKJV

You, too, can do *"strange things"* in Jesus' name. Use your God-given authority. Stop waiting for feelings, and build your faith in the Word of God:

Inasmuch then as the children have partaken of flesh and blood, He Himself likewise shared in the same, that through death He might destroy him who had the power of death, that is, the devil, and release those who through fear of death

> *were all their lifetime subject to bondage.* Hebrews 2:14-15, NKJV

Redemption puts you in command, even of death:

> *I am He who lives, and was dead, and behold, I am alive forevermore. Amen. And I have the keys of Hades and of Death.* Revelation 1:18, NKJV

All things are now possible to you by and through the power of the Holy Spirit.

THE SACRED ANOINTING OIL

The ministry of the anointing oil is a mystery of the Kingdom for the elevation of the saints. The sacred oil was initiated by God Himself:

> *And thou shalt speak unto the children of Israel, saying, This shall be an holy anointing oil unto me throughout your generations.* Exodus 30:31

This is truth, not an opinion. Kings were enthroned with the use of this oil. It is the key to enthronement:

> *And the destruction of Ahaziah was of God by coming to Joram: for when he was come, he went out with Jehoram against Jehu the son of Nimshi, whom the LORD had anointed to cut off the house of Ahab.* 2 Chronicles 22:7

This oil can bring a complete end to the wickedness around you, cutting it off:

> *And it shall come to pass in that day, that his burden shall be taken away from off thy shoulder, and his yoke from off thy neck, and the yoke shall be destroyed because of the anointing.*
> Isaiah 10:27

> *Is any sick among you? let him call for the elders of the church; and let them pray over him, anointing him with oil in the name of the Lord: and the prayer*

of faith shall save the sick, and the Lord shall raise him up; and if he have committed sins, they shall be forgiven him.
James 5:1415

The oil separates things and people to God, making them holy:

And thou shalt anoint the tabernacle of the congregation therewith, and the ark of the testimony, and the table and all his vessels, and the candlestick and his vessels, and the altar of incense, and the altar of burnt offering with all his vessels, and the laver and his foot. And thou shalt sanctify them, that they may be most holy: whatsoever toucheth them shall be holy. Exodus 30:26-29

This is why when you are anointed with oil, the sickness that touches you becomes holy, so it loses its wickedness, and you are healed.

What does anointing oil do? Here are some highlights:

1. The Oil Provokes an Instant Manifestation of Good News by the Power of God

Then Samuel took a vial of oil, and poured it upon his head, and kissed him, and said, Is it not because the Lord hath anointed thee to be captain over his inheritance? 1 Samuel 10:1

Through the anointing oil, your concerns turn to testimony, whatever you have been waiting for is delivered, and you come to the end of your sorrows. With the anointing oil, there is an instant fulfillment of prophecy:

So it was, when he had turned his back to go from Samuel, that God gave him another heart; and all those signs came to pass that day.
1 Samuel 10:9, NKJV

*It shall come to pass in that day
That his burden will be taken away from your shoulder,*

*And his yoke from your neck,
And the yoke will be destroyed because of the anointing oil.*
       Isaiah 10:27, NKJV

Your day of total freedom has come.

2. The Oil Enforces a Supernatural Change of the Story

The supremacy of God goes into action when the anointing oil is put on you and as you respond to it in faith:

Then the Spirit of the Lord will come upon you, and you will prophesy with them and be turned into another man. When they came there to the hill, there was a group of prophets to meet him; then the Spirit of God came upon him, and he prophesied among them. And it happened, when all who knew him formerly saw that he indeed prophesied among the prophets, that the people said

> *to one another, "What is this that has come upon the son of Kish? Is Saul also among the prophets?"*
>
> *Then a man from there answered and said, "But who is their father?" Therefore it became a proverb: "Is Saul also among the prophets?"*
>
> 1 Samuel 10:6 and 10-12, NKJV

This is the day for your change of status. Jesus Christ is the same yesterday, today, and forever.

3. THE OIL BRINGS TOTAL RESTORATION

Whatever you have lost is restored:

> *When you have departed from me today, you will find two men by Rachel's tomb in the territory of Benjamin at Zelzah; and they will say to you, 'The donkeys which you went to look for have been found. And now your father has ceased caring about the donkeys and*

is worrying about you, saying, "What shall I do about my son?"
1 Samuel 10:2 NKJV

"The donkeys which you went to search for have been found." Your health has been found, your job has been found, your promotion has been found, your breakthrough has been found, your joy and peace has been found in the name of Jesus Christ. It is restoration time.

4. THE OIL BRINGS YOU DIVINE FAVOR

And they will greet you and give you two loaves of bread, which you shall receive from their hands.
1 Samuel 10:4, NKJV

"They will greet you and give you" when you don't deserve something and you don't even know that it is available, but it suddenly jumps on you, that's called favor. Two men had three loaves of bread (verse 3), but they

gave you two of them. They were ready to sacrifice to meet your need, even though they didn't even know you. Wow! God is arranging favor for you this week in Jesus' name:

> *You love righteousness and hate wickedness;*
> *Therefore God, Your God, has anointed You*
> *With the oil of gladness more than Your companions.*
> *All Your garments are scented with myrrh and aloes and cassia,*
> *Out of the ivory palaces, by which they have made You glad.*
>
> Psalm 45:7-8, NKJV

> *Then Samuel took the horn of oil and anointed him in the midst of his brothers; and the Spirit of the* LORD *came upon David from that day forward. So Samuel arose and went to Ramah.*
>
> 1 Samuel 16:13, NKJV

> *And so it was, whenever the spirit from God was upon Saul, that David would*

take a harp and play it with his hand. Then Saul would become refreshed and well, and the distressing spirit would depart from him. 1 Samuel 16:23, NKJV

With the result of the anointing oil in your life, favor will come looking for you. Thank God for His favors and blessings. *"It is written."* Amen!

- Father, I give You thanks, for I am anointed, I am holy, and everything that touches me from today on becomes holy.
- Father, in the name of Jesus Christ, by this anointing, I curse the root of every wickedness around me. Cease in Jesus' name!
- I command now, as I am commanded, favor, locate me now. Peace, joy, promotion, come to me. This week my destiny is fulfilled in Jesus' name.

The world has yet to see the emergence of such strange men and women living on Earth. Our manifestation and proofs will amaze the world because of the Spirit of God living in us. Heaven will be real on Earth again. God will manifest His glory through the name of Jesus Christ. Men and women will fear and be in anguish because of the mighty acts of God through the Body of Christ:

> *To the intent that now the manifold wisdom of God might be made known by the church to the principalities and powers in the heavenly places.*
> Ephesians 3:10, NKJV

This is living a supernatural life that cannot be faulted:

> *I tell you the truth, anyone who believes in me will do the same works I have done, and even greater works, because I am going to be with the Father.*
> John 14:12, NLT

When you are right with God, everything flows to you because you are in Christ, and in Christ all the fullness of God dwells:

For in Christ lives all the fullness of God in a human body. So you also are complete through your union with Christ, who is the head over every ruler and authority. Colossians 2:9-10, NLT

Your new life is one of solutions. The Law and all its consequences lost its place when Jesus died:

For Christ is the end of the law for righteousness to every one that believeth.
Romans 10:4

The law of sin and death came to an end because all that caused it had been judged in and through Christ. Now there is no Law and no judgment, and since there is no Law, there can be no punishment:

Yet we know that a person is made right with God by faith in Jesus Christ, not by obeying the law. And we have believed in Christ Jesus, so that we might be made right with God because

> *of our faith in Christ, not because we have obeyed the law. For no one will ever be made right with God by obeying the law.*
>
> *I do not treat the grace of God as meaningless. For if keeping the law could make us right with God, then there was no need for Christ to die.*
>
> Galatians 2:16 and 21, NLT

Because of Christ, no one can stand against you and me and survive. There is an irrevocable blessing upon us that guarantees victory always:

> *Dear brothers and sisters, here's an example from everyday life. Just as no one can set aside or amend an irrevocable agreement, so it is in this case. God gave the promises to Abraham and his child. And notice that the Scripture doesn't say "to his children," as if it meant many descendants. Rather, it says "to his child" and that, of course, means Christ.*   Galatians 3:15-6, NLT

> *Thus saith the Lord, As the new wine is found in the cluster, and one saith, Destroy it not; for a blessing is in it: so will I do for my servants' sakes, that I may not destroy them all.* Isaiah 65:8

He says, *"Destroy it not; for a blessing is in it."* Paul wrote:

> *And if children, then heirs; heirs of God, and joint-heirs with Christ; if so be that we suffer with him, that we may be also glorified together.* Romans 8:17

This brings us into the picture. There is an irrevocable blessing on your life today. You can walk in wonders. How? Here are some keys to receiving miracles from God:

1. Be Fascinated by the Word of God

Miracles happen when the Word of God is preached in truth:

> *But the unbelieving Jews stirred up the Gentiles, and made their minds evil affected against the brethren. Long time therefore abode they speaking boldly in the Lord, which gave testimony unto the word of his grace, and granted signs and wonders to be done by their hands.*
> Acts 14:2-3

The Word shows you what is available, and you can then walk into it because you know it's real:

> *And straightway many were gathered together, insomuch that there was no room to receive them, no, not so much as about the door: and he preached the word unto them.* Mark 2:2

Jesus was revealing what is available to everyone in the Kingdom. Never forget, the Kingdom of God is a system God designed to satisfy all its citizens. As noted, Jesus said your heavenly Father knows you have need of these things. If you act on the Word, you will dwell in the midst of miracles.

As Jesus preached the Word to the crowd gathered in a house, a man with palsy who was being carried in by some friends sensed that there was hope for him that very day. I strongly believe that what drew these people was what they were hearing.

2. You Need Helpers of Destiny Who Think Like You Do

If you don't have a dream, you can't walk in wonders. You're just wasting resources. But God is set to do something, about your desire:

> *Be not ye therefore like unto them: for your Father knoweth what things ye have need of, before ye ask him.*
>
> Matthew 6:8

God is limitless, He has no boundaries, and there can be no resistance to fulfilling His plans. He said, "Who will be a brier or a thorn in My way?" You dare not do that. But if people around you are vision killers, they can kill your faith by their ideas for doing things that are contrary to God's way of doing things.

Naaman had a way he thought would bring him healing. He was looking to the good rivers around Damascus. But that was not the way. You need to be surrounded by people of desperate faith.

Verses 3 and 4 of Mark 2 show that people carried this needy man with a desperation of faith and an unwillingness to take no for an answer. After all, Jesus was in that place. The work could be done now. They must have been saying to the man on the stretcher, "Today is your day. Whatever it takes, we will be there for you."

Thank God for your faith, but you need a right environment in order for it to thrive.

3. Never Mind the Obstacles

There is always room for you if you press in (see Mark 2:4). There is no obstacle that can stop your faith and desire. Whatever stands before you today is temporal. Don't make it permanent by giving it a name.

The people who carried this man could not get in because of the crowd. Why was it that the rest of the crowd didn't have a testimony, just this one man? He was the one who was determined to ignore the obstacles and go for his miracle.

It has been said, "Nobody can make it in a pandemic." Says who? You don't know how many people might be amazed in the crowd if you don't always look for the obstacle. If you don't mind the obstacle, divine wisdom will come to you, and God will make a way.

4. Take the Step of Faith As You Are Led By the Spirit and Do the Unusual

Your life is not an experiment. God wants to make you a living wonder. Without supernatural life, your Christianity will lose its flavor. You must take a step of faith now, as these men did. Your step of faith must be divinely directed because of your desperation. Jesus is right there with you today. Why should your friend go home with palsy when Jesus had the answer?

After your healing, you can get a job and pay for the roof repairs. God is right there if you want His touch.

Big faith produces big miracles. When the Spirit of God is leading you, dare anything. Dance unusually! Praise unusually! Give unusually! Pray unusually! Do something extraordinary by the leading of the Spirit.

5. Set Your Eyes on Jesus, and Your Life Will Never Be the Same Again

The attention that day was not on what people thought or felt or even on the situation this man was going through. It was all about Jesus. In Mark 2:5, Jesus saw their faith. This kind of faith is visible. It's notable. He didn't see their cry; He saw their faith. Why? Because their eyes were on Him. When your attention is on Him, He sees you.

What the palsied man had come for he needed now, so he was let down through the roof before Jesus. And God is visiting you today, no matter your need.

6. Release Your Faith in God's Love for You, and Wonders Will Erupt

It's not about how desperate you are to see Jesus, but how deeply you know you are loved. Jesus didn't say anything about the roof being torn up and the protocol being breached. He was concerned about the health of this man. He loves you, and He can't stand to see you in pain.

Jesus called this man *"Son."* His major assignment was to destroy the works of the devil, so each time He saw the devil in operation, He jumped in to bring restoration.

God doesn't love you just because you're a Christian; He loved you even when you were a sinner:

> *But God commendeth his love toward us, in that, while we were yet sinners, Christ died for us.* Romans 5:8

You received that love by becoming a Christian, and He put His own life, nature and Spirit in you, so that you could live a life of wonders.

Believe the Lord. Wonders are here now because He is here. Take what you need now because it's for you. You are loved and love gives. Whatever your desires are, receive them now in Jesus' name.

> *Herein is love, not that we loved God, but that he loved us, and sent his Son to be the propitiation for our sins.*
> 1 John 4:10

7. YOUR SINS ARE FORGIVEN, SO YOU CANNOT CARRY YOUR SHAME AND REPROACH ANYMORE

Jesus attacked the root of the problem (see Mark 2:5-12). The foundation for every oppression is sin. All of mankind became victims because of the sin in the garden of Eden:

> *For as by one man's disobedience many were made sinners, so by the obedience of one shall many be made righteous.*
> Romans 5:19

We were dead through that sin. Death and sickness, failure and frustration came through sin. There can be no freedom without the sin issue being resolved. It pleased God to make Jesus the Offering for sin. You must see this and believe this to experience miracles. Your sins are forgiven and taken away as if they had never existed. This is a mystery beyond human understanding:

> *If we confess our sins, he is faithful and just to forgive us our sins, and to cleanse us from all unrighteousness.* 1 John 1:9

> *And, behold, they brought to him a man sick of the palsy, lying on a bed: and*

> *Jesus seeing their faith said unto the sick of the palsy; Son, be of good cheer; thy sins be forgiven thee.*
> *And he arose, and departed to his house.* Matthew 9:2 and 7

You are forgiven. Therefore, also be healed now. Receive your breakthrough today:

> *Repent ye therefore, and be converted, that your sins may be blotted out, when the times of refreshing shall come from the presence of the Lord.* Acts 3:19

Yes, when you have secured your future in Christ, you can start *Ruling Your World*.

Chapter 6

Unlocking Unlimited Wonders

For by grace are ye saved through faith; and that not of yourselves: it is the gift of God: not of works, lest any man should boast.   Ephesians 2:8-9

Living a life of wonders is complicated if you don't know what God did for us in and through Christ Jesus. We have been totally restored to the Eden model. This is not something that you and I planned; it is the doing of God to achieve His purpose and dream for humanity.

Paul called this a work of grace. Our calling is not a nomenclature, and it's not a mere title. Our calling is a divine commission to power and rulership:

> *But as many as received him, to them gave he power to become the sons of God, even to them that believe on his name.*
> John 1:12

The demonstration of our calling gives us dominion over Satan, sickness and disease, lack, and even death. We are deployed by God to show the superiority of Heaven over the Earth:

> *Then he called his twelve disciples together, and gave them power and authority over all devils, and to cure diseases. And he sent them to preach the Kingdom of God, and to heal the sick. And he said unto them, Take nothing for your journey, neither staves, nor scrip, neither bread, neither money; neither have two coats apiece. And whatsoever house ye enter into, there abide, and thence depart. And whosoever will not*

receive you, when ye go out of that city, shake off the very dust from your feet for a testimony against them. Luke 9:1-5

And he ordained twelve, that they should be with him, and that he might send them forth to preach, and to have power to heal sicknesses, and to cast out devils. Mark 3:14-15

Until you take the words of Jesus as an impartation of power, you will not see the demonstration of His glory in your daily life:

And they were astonished at his doctrine: for his word was with power.
Luke 4:32

A child is conceived through the male and female gametes coming together. Nobody doubts that. The new creation is conceived by the coming of the Spirit of God into our spirit. There is a divine conception that takes place. Suddenly our body becomes a host of this new being. Too many people don't see that because it's a spiritual thing:

> *But as many as received him, to them gave he power to become the sons of God, even to them that believe on his name: which were born, not of blood, nor of the will of the flesh, nor of the will of man, but of God.* John 1:12-13

Jesus said it this way:

> *The wind bloweth where it listeth, and thou hearest the sound thereof, but canst not tell whence it cometh, and whither it goeth: so is every one that is born of the Spirit.* John 3:8

You are an airborne miracle, unstoppable and irresistible, and that is why the Scriptures declare:

> *Behold, I and the children whom the* L*ORD* *hath given me are for signs and*

for wonders in Israel from the LORD of hosts, which dwelleth in mount Zion.
Isaiah 8:18

"*I and the children ... .*" He grouped us with Himself. Therefore, every reason given for failure is a demonstration of ignorance:

When I consider thy Heavens, the work of thy fingers, the moon and the stars, which thou hast ordained; what is man, that thou art mindful of him? and the son of man, that thou visitest him? For thou hast made him a little lower than the angels, and hast crowned him with glory and honour. Thou madest him to have dominion over the works of thy hands; thou hast put all things under his feet. Psalm 8:3-6

This is the truth of what God created. In Christ, you become unstoppable by any contrary force. What could not stop Jesus Christ also cannot stop you. God wanted Christ to reign on Earth, and that is the only thing that will make the Earth like Heaven. This is what we are translated into when we are saved, and we are saved to become creative wonders on the Earth:

> *Therefore let no man glory in men. For all things are yours; whether Paul, or Apollos, or Cephas, or the world, or life, or death, or things present, or things to come; all are yours; and ye are Christ's; and Christ is God's.* 1 Corinthians 3:21-23

We are Christ's and Christ is God's. That mentality brings you to a place of talking to the mountains and trees and cancer and coronavirus, knowing that they must obey you. I'm not talking about your flesh; I'm talking about the you that is made in the image of Christ. Don't let that body of yours deceive you. There is a giant inside. Your spirit is stronger than your physical body, so don't rate yourself by what you see or feel.

This is your introduction into a whole new world, and in this world, failure is not an option:

Who hath delivered us from the power of darkness, and hath translated us into the kingdom of his dear Son.
Colossians 1:13

With the new birth, there are many things that you can and should enjoy:

1. You Are Connected to the Throne of Grace

Let us therefore come boldly unto the throne of grace, that we may obtain mercy, and find grace to help in time of need. Hebrews 4:16

Everyone under the Old Covenant had to come through the High Priest, and a sacrifice had to be made. Otherwise, death was the result. Nadab and Abihu went into the presence of God without being invited, and they died. But today you have the nature of God in you, and you are righteous by the blood that washed you. Therefore, you can come boldly to God. He certifies you competent to have access to His very court. So go on, by faith, take what you need.

Nothing ever dies in that place:

> *And Moses laid up the rods before the LORD in the tabernacle of witness. And it came to pass, that on the morrow Moses went into the tabernacle of witness; and, behold, the rod of Aaron for the house of Levi was budded, and brought forth buds, and bloomed blossoms, and yielded almonds.* Numbers 17:7-8

The rod of Aaron budded and produced fruit overnight, and the same thing is happening to you now in Jesus' name. Because your spirit is reborn, the Spirit of the living God is poured into your spirit, and you can know what God knows:

> *And because ye are sons, God hath sent forth the Spirit of his Son into your hearts, crying, Abba, Father. Wherefore thou art no more a servant, but a son; and if a son, then an heir of God through Christ.* Galatians 4:6-7

Remember, if you are a son, you must be heard (see Matthew 17:15).

2. You Have Access To Divine Instruction and Direction

The key to wonders and results is divine direction and guidance. Many fail in life, not because they are sinning or because of the devil, but because they don't know any better:

> *The labour of the foolish wearieth every one of them, because he knoweth not how to go to the city.*
> Ecclesiastes 10:15

Your new birth gives you access to what the Spirit is saying because your spirit is connected to the Spirit of God inside you:

> *For as many as are led by the Spirit of God, they are the sons of God. For ye have not received the spirit of bondage again to fear; but ye have received the*

> *Spirit of adoption, whereby we cry, Abba, Father. The Spirit itself beareth witness with our spirit, that we are the children of God.* Romans 8:14-16

> *He that believeth on me, as the scripture hath said, out of his belly shall flow rivers of living water. (But this spake he of the Spirit, which they that believe on him should receive: for the Holy Ghost was not yet given; because that Jesus was not yet glorified.)* John 7:38-39

> *But there is a spirit in man: and the inspiration of the Almighty giveth them understanding.* Job 32:8

> *The spirit of man is the candle of the LORD, searching all the inward parts of the belly.* Proverbs 20:27

There are ideas, concepts, and insights that God wants to pass along to you as an extension of His omnipotence, in order for new things to manifest in your life. Your spirit can catch them, but your mind must be ready to take them in as well.

3. This Connects You with Your Potential

You are born with so much value that it's impossible for you to lose that value. You're a treasure:

> *But we have this treasure in earthen vessels, that the excellency of the power may be of God, and not of us.*
> 2 Corinthians 4:7

Everything created by God came from parent materials that determines their function and potential. The fish came from water, and water is their strength. The animals came from the earth, and the earth sustains them. They live in the woods with no fear. You can't live there because you're not designed for it. Man came from God and must be sustained by Him. The nature of God is in him. Therefore, He has all the attributes and character of God in him.

Paul said it this way:

> *I can do all things through Christ who strengthens me.*
> Philippians 4:13, NKJV

You can't live without results because that's the way you are wired to function. Cain was cursed:

> *When thou tillest the ground, it shall not henceforth yield unto thee her strength; a fugitive and a vagabond shalt thou be in the earth. And Cain said unto the LORD, My punishment is greater than I can bear.*
> *And Cain knew his wife; and she conceived, and bare Enoch: and he builded a city, and called the name of the city, after the name of his son, Enoch.*
> Genesis 4:12-13, and 17

Even though Cain was cursed, the potential was still there. The nature of God was in him. You are blessed, so how much more should you manifest wonders in the name of Jesus Christ:

> *Verily, verily, I say unto you, He that believeth on me, the works that I do shall he do also; and greater works than these shall he do; because I go unto my Father.* John 14:12

It's time to start doing those *"greater works"* and glorifying God in your life.

Many are born again but never experience wonders. Why? Because Matthew 6:33 is not taken into consideration. Seek Him first and the wonders will manifest in Jesus' name.

We are redeemed as living wonders:

> *But as many as received him, to them gave he power to become the sons of God, even to them that believe on his name.* John 1:12

You cannot become a child of God and not walk in authority and power. He has conferred on us authority and power like our Father has.

Ruling Your World

By the Law of Creation, like begets like. A dog can only give birth to a dog, a cat to a cat, and a bird to a bird, each one after its own kind. God can only give birth to a god:

> *For in him we live, and move, and have our being; as certain also of your own poets have said, For we are also his offspring.* Acts 17:28

"We are His offspring." Therefore, we can speak to things and get results is our ordained position in Christ Jesus. Everything is designed to obey us. Jesus said:

> *For verily I say unto you, That whosoever shall say unto this mountain, Be thou removed, and be thou cast into the sea; and shall not doubt in his heart, but shall believe that those things which he saith shall come to pass; he shall have whatsoever he saith.* Mark 11:23

> *And the Lord said, If ye had faith as a grain of mustard seed, ye might say*

> *unto this sycamine tree, Be thou plucked up by the root, and be thou planted in the sea; and it should obey you.*
> Luke 17:6

This was what Adam did to the animals (see Genesis 2:19). Everything became what he called it.

When you came into this family, you came as a king. Kings don't rule by advice and opinion; kings rule by decree. *"You will decree a thing, and it shall be established"*:

> *Thou shalt also decree a thing, and it shall be established unto thee: and the light shall shine upon thy ways.* Job 22:28

God makes you do that. *"Where the word of a king is, there is power"*:

> *Where the word of a king is, there is power: and who may say unto him, What doest thou?* Ecclesiastes 8:4

> *And they sung a new song, saying, Thou art worthy to take the book, and*

> *to open the seals thereof: for thou wast slain, and hast redeemed us to God by thy blood out of every kindred, and tongue, and people, and nation; and hast made us unto our God kings and priests: and we shall reign on the earth.*
>
> Revelation 5:9-10

Yes, you are a king. God's view of a king is different from man's view:

> *And the LORD said unto Samuel, Hearken unto the voice of the people in all that they say unto thee: for they have not rejected thee, but they have rejected me, that I should not reign over them. According to all the works which they have done since the day that I brought them up out of Egypt even unto this day, wherewith they have forsaken me, and served other gods, so do they also unto thee. Now therefore hearken unto their voice: howbeit yet protest solemnly unto them, and shew them the manner of the king that shall reign over them.*

And Samuel told all the words of the LORD unto the people that asked of him a king. And he said, This will be the manner of the king that shall reign over you: He will take your sons, and appoint them for himself, for his chariots, and to be his horsemen; and some shall run before his chariots. And he will appoint him captains over thousands, and captains over fifties; and will set them to ear his ground, and to reap his harvest, and to make his instruments of war, and instruments of his chariots. And he will take your daughters to be confectionaries, and to be cooks, and to be bakers. And he will take your fields, and your vineyards, and your oliveyards, even the best of them, and give them to his servants. And he will take the tenth of your seed, and of your vineyards, and give to his officers, and to his servants. And he will take your menservants, and your maidservants, and your goodliest young men, and your asses, and put them to his work. He will take the tenth of your

> *sheep: and ye shall be his servants. And ye shall cry out in that day because of your king which ye shall have chosen you; and the LORD will not hear you in that day.*
>
> *Nevertheless the people refused to obey the voice of Samuel; and they said, Nay; but we will have a king over us.*
>
> 1 Samuel 8:7-19

The value God has placed on you is the reason He created you in His image. There is nothing that He did not put in you to be like Him. However, your continual manifestation of power and authority depends on your trust and complete obedience to His Word and your righteous lifestyle.

God told Adam and Eve, *"The day you eat the fruit of the tree of knowledge of good and evil, you will surely die"*:

> *But of the tree of the knowledge of good and evil, thou shalt not eat of it: for in the day that thou eatest thereof thou shalt surely die.* Genesis 2:17

Death comes by disobeying the Word of God. Then, however, the devil came too, and he said something very different: *"You will not surely die"*:

> *And the serpent said unto the woman, Ye shall not surely die.* Genesis 3:4

Unfortunately, Adam and Eve trusted the other voice, and they died. In the New Testament, God said, *"I give you power over serpent and scorpions"*:

> *Behold, I give unto you power to tread on serpents and scorpions, and over all the power of the enemy: and nothing shall by any means hurt you.* Luke 10:19

If you say you don't have that power, you are agreeing with the enemy who says, "You're too weak." God said, *"Whatsoever he doeth shall prosper"*:

> *And he shall be like a tree planted by the rivers of water, that bringeth forth his*

> *fruit in his season; his leaf also shall not wither; and whatsoever he doeth shall prosper.* Psalm 1:3

He has promised to supply all you need:

> *But my God shall supply all your need according to his riches in glory by Christ Jesus.* Philippians 4:19

"But," you might say, "nothing is working for me." Maybe you gave away your authority to the enemy and took death instead of life.

It's all about trust. Either it makes sense or it doesn't. The deterioration in the life of man is caused by his inability to agree with God based on His Word:

> *Say unto them, As truly as I live, saith the LORD, as ye have spoken in mine ears, so will I do to you.* Numbers 14:28

Doubting the Word is saying, "God has no integrity. He doesn't really mean what

He says. "That's awkward. Step out in faith now, for you have authority over every situation on Earth. That means you can dream big and obtain what you dream.

You have become the elect of God because of Jesus. It is the forgiveness of sin that changed your status and put authority on your lips. Now use it! Here are some important keys:

1. You Have A Unique Seat of Power that Rules Over All Things

Since you have been raised to new life with Christ, set your sights on the realities of heaven, where Christ sits in the place of honor at God's right hand.
And when Christ, who is your life, is revealed to the whole world, you will share in all his glory.
                    Colossians 3:1 and 4, NLT

When Heaven's thoughts fill your mind, you will experience the manifestation of power and authority that makes you a wonder in the Earth. In Christ, you have experienced a restoration of dignity and influence because He has reconnected you with the Father with all the privileges of the throne of God:

> *Even when we were dead in trespasses, [God] made us alive together with Christ (by grace you have been saved), and raised us up together, and made us sit together in the heavenly places in Christ Jesus.* Ephesians 2:6, NKJV

We are now commissioned by God to represent Him and the government of Heaven here on the Earth:

> *He who hears you hears Me, he who rejects you rejects Me, and he who rejects Me rejects Him who sent Me.*
> Luke 10:16, NKJV

It is all through what Jesus did on the cross. We now have intimacy with the Creator, and daily guidance from Him. But you must choose to believe it to see it happen:

> *Don't you realize that your body is the temple of the Holy Spirit, who lives in you and was given to you by God? You do not belong to yourself, for God bought you with a high price. So you must honor God with your body.*
> 1 Corinthians 6:19-20, NLT

2. You Have the Word of the Living God

God created everything through him,
  and nothing was created except through him.
The Word gave life to everything that was created,
  and his life brought light to everyone.
The light shines in the darkness,
  and the darkness can never extinguish it. John 1:3-5, NLT

God's Word is not just a message or an idea; it is a Person. It is a creative force. It's a tool to change and alter things in the whole Universe. There are things we no longer enjoy, not because that is what the Word created, but because of the Fall. What makes things alive is the life they have in them. Without this life, they're dead. The Word puts life into everything that was created.

When perverted, the life is still there, but it starts to work to the contrary. It now works to prevent that thing from living, and life is withdrawn from it. That is why God has given you authority, and the Word is the tool that facilitates that authority.

In the beginning, every virus that was created was for our good. It was only after things were perverted that viruses became killers. They are sometimes very powerful, but we have authority through Christ Jesus to take the life out of them. Then they become powerless.

When Daniel was in the lion's den, it was not that the lions were not hungry. They

Unlocking Unlimited Wonders

couldn't eat him. He was too powerful. The Bible says he prayed, and the Lord sent an angel and *"stopped the mouths of the lions"* (Daniel 6:22).

We have been looking at Paul the apostle on the island of Melita. Here it is again:

> *As Paul gathered an armful of sticks and was laying them on the fire, a poisonous snake, driven out by the heat, bit him on the hand. The people of the island saw it hanging from his hand and said to each other, "A murderer, no doubt! Though he escaped the sea, justice will not permit him to live." But Paul shook off the snake into the fire and was unharmed. The people waited for him to swell up or suddenly drop dead. But when they had waited a long time and saw that he wasn't harmed, they changed their minds and decided he was a god.* Acts 28:3-6, NLT

It's your turn to shake off what wants to harm you. You have that authority right now in Christ through the Word of God.

Meditate on that Word, declare it, believe it, and see the glory of God shine.

A Centurion said to Jesus, "Just speak a word and that will take life out of the sickness, and my servant will be healed. I know You, Jesus. You are the Word of the living God":

> *But the officer said, "Lord, I am not worthy to have you come into my home. Just say the word from where you are, and my servant will be healed."*
> Matthew 8:8, NLT

As we have seen, Jesus said that just as the Father sent Him, He was sending us:

> *Again he said, "Peace be with you. As the Father has sent me, so I am sending you."* John 20:21, NLT

Stop giving the devil any space at all. You are the mouthpiece of the Almighty on Earth. You are part of a Kingdom of priests unto God:

And ye shall be unto me a kingdom of priests, and an holy nation. These are the words which thou shalt speak unto the children of Israel.   Exodus 19:6

First Peter 2:9 declares that we are a royal priesthood. Speak now! That is your privilege. You have the backing of Almighty God if you will believe Him.

- Father, in the name of Jesus, I take power over this virus today. Virus, be powerless over me. We paralyze you over America in the name of Jesus Christ.
- Father, in the name of Jesus Christ, I decree now that favor be planted firmly in my life. Mountains of frustration, be removed now.

Now, you create something. Cry out to God. Remove things you don't want in your life in Jesus' name. Create for yourself, your husband, your wife, your children. Create something with your words. The Holy Spirit will do the rest.

Amen!

The entry point into the covenant of God is marked with success:

> *But as many as received him, to them gave he power to become the sons of God, even to them that believe on his name,*
> John 1:12

> *For whatsoever is born of God overcometh the world: and this is the victory that overcometh the world, even our faith. Who is he that overcometh the world, but he that believeth that Jesus is the Son of God?* 1 John 5:4-5

> *And if ye be Christ's, then are ye Abraham's seed, and heirs according to the promise.* Galatians 3:29

This marks the end of failure and frustration in your life in the name of Jesus Christ.

God wants you to share in the same success He gave to all covenant people. That's why He gave you His nature.

Equality for man with God was the agenda for creation. It was in the original blueprint. In fact, the Bible says that we should conform to the image of His dear Son:

> *For whom he did foreknow, he also did predestinate to be conformed to the image of his Son, that he might be the firstborn among many brethren.*
> Romans 8:29

> *The first man is of the earth, earthy: the second man is the Lord from heaven. As is the earthy, such are they also that are earthy: and as is the heavenly, such are they also that are heavenly. And as we have borne the image of the earthy, we shall also bear the image of the heavenly.*
> 1 Corinthians 15:47-49

Yes, if we bear the image of the earthy, we shall also bear the image of the heavenly.

We are bearing the image of Jesus Christ, He who lived in a human body to prove that God could successfully inhabit a man. But even though He operated as a man, He is God. He was the Pattern Son:

> *Then said Jesus to them again, Peace be unto you: as my Father hath sent me, even so send I you.* John 20:21

Yes, He took the form of man:

> *But made himself of no reputation, and took upon him the form of a servant, and was made in the likeness of men: and being found in fashion as a man, he humbled himself, and became obedient unto death, even the death of the cross.*
> Philippians 2:7-8

You, too, can take on a heavenly form through the power of the Holy Spirit who resides in you. You cannot be on God's level without having His nature in you:

> *Whereby are given unto us exceeding great and precious promises: that by these ye might be partakers of the divine nature, having escaped the corruption that is in the world through lust.*
>
> 2 Peter 1:4

> *If so be ye have tasted that the Lord is gracious.* 1 Peter 2:3

We are partaker of His divine nature? How can that be? Because we have become the righteousness of God in Christ:

> *For He made Him who knew no sin to be sin for us, that we might become the righteousness of God in Him.*
>
> 2 Corinthians 5:21, NKJV

The peak of living wonders in life is found in the essence of the blood of Jesus Christ washing us clean as if sin had never existed in us and connecting us back to God to live like Christ here on Earth:

> *In Him also we have obtained an inheritance, being predestined according to the purpose of Him who works all things according to the counsel of His will, that we who first trusted in Christ should be to the praise of His glory. In Him you also trusted, after you heard the word of truth, the gospel of your salvation; in whom also, having believed, you were sealed with the Holy Spirit of promise.*
> Ephesians 1:11-13, NKJV

Now we also have the mind of Christ:

> *For "who has known the mind of the Lord that he may instruct Him?" But we have the mind of Christ.*
> 1 Corinthians 2:16, NKJV

That exceptional mind gives us an unparalleled thinking ability that results in unusual success. Salvation reveals the righteousness of God by making us new, like Adam and Eve before they sinned:

> *To all who are in Rome, beloved of God, called to be saints:*
>
> *Grace to you and peace from God our Father and the Lord Jesus Christ.*
>
> *For I am not ashamed of the gospel of Christ, for it is the power of God to salvation for everyone who believes, for the Jew first and also for the Greek. For in it the righteousness of God is revealed from faith to faith; as it is written, "The just shall live by faith."*
>
> Romans 1:7 and 16-17, NKJV

The restoration of man back to God is the foundation for success and fellowship and the extermination of failure. God want us to enjoy the same fellowship He has with Jesus Christ:

> *God is faithful, by whom you were called into the fellowship of His Son, Jesus Christ our Lord.*   1 Corinthians 1:9, NKJV

As we talk to and with our Creator, believing and acting on His Word, the center of everything being Jesus Christ, He gives us peace, joy, and fulfillment in life:

> *Jesus, knowing that the Father had given all things into His hands, and that He had come from God and was going to God ...* John 13:3, NKJV

In the same way, the Father has given all things into our hands.

Satan recognized Jesus, all of nature recognized Him, and the sea recognized Him and bowed before Him. Righteousness makes all the difference and it will make everything bow to you too.

Nature knew what many believers don't yet know. And wherever and whatever Jesus Christ mastered, we, too, can master. Righteousness is a masterful thing, and it is a gift from Jesus Christ to you and me. He paid the full price for it:

> *Therefore, having been justified by faith, we have peace with God through our Lord Jesus Christ.* Romans 5:17, NKJV

The moment you declare your righteousness, Satan loses all strength and every weapon over you. In that moment, he knows you are taking the position of Jesus, and he can no longer overcome you. Why? Because righteousness is your covering:

> *Arise, O LORD, into thy rest; thou, and the ark of thy strength. Let thy priests be clothed with righteousness; and let thy saints shout for joy.*
> Psalm 132:8-9

> *I will greatly rejoice in the LORD,*
> *My soul shall be joyful in my God;*
> *For He has clothed me with the garments of salvation,*
> *He has covered me with the robe of righteousness,*
> *As a bridegroom decks himself with ornaments,*
> *And as a bride adorns herself with her jewels.*
> *For as the earth brings forth its bud,*
> *As the garden causes the things that are*

> *sown in it to spring forth,*
> *So the Lord God will cause righteousness and praise to spring forth before all the nations.* Isaiah 61:10-11, NKJV

What Christ now is is what we now are, not what we should be, nor what we could be:

> *Love has been perfected among us in this: that we may have boldness in the day of judgment; because as He is, so are we in this world.*
> 1 John 4:17, NKJV

This concept is not taught nearly enough in churches today. Most Christians seem to be living by chance. That's not God's way. Is Jesus Christ in sin? Can He be sick? Can He lack anything? Of course not. So declare that none of these things will affect you either.

Here's another promise you need to meditate on:

> *You are of God, little children, and have overcome them, because He who is in*

you is greater than he who is in the world.   1 John 4:4, NKJV

That is the Word of God, and it means that you have superiority over everything on Earth. Your presence is intimidating to all the forces of darkness. Since God is with us and in us, there is nothing we cannot overcome. The Greater One in us is superior to everything else.

This is the force that conquers cancer and infections, viruses, and abnormal blood pressure. For the believer, these things must end now. Jesus is reclaiming His property.

Your inheritance in Christ is shining brightly, and that is the foundation you need for success in life:

Then the righteous will shine forth as the sun in the kingdom of their Father. He who has ears to hear, let him hear!
                      Matthew 13:43, NKJV

So, start dreaming. Put your vision out there. What would you do or say if you knew you could not fail, you could not be stopped, you could no longer be oppressed, and whatever you said would come true? Then say it now! Believe it now in Jesus' name:

> *Confess your sins to each other and pray for each other so that you may be healed. The earnest prayer of a righteous person has great power and produces wonderful results.* James 5:16, NLT

God is the Judge, He is the Justifier, and He presents us to Himself without blemish, without wrinkle, and without condemnation. That, my friends, is the peak of successful living. You and I are living wonders in this world:

> *And the work of righteousness shall be peace; and the effect of righteousness quietness and assurance for ever. And my people shall dwell in a peaceable habitation, and in sure dwellings, and in quiet resting places; when it shall hail, coming down on the forest; and the city shall be low in a low place.* Isaiah 32:17-19

Unlocking Unlimited Wonders

And this righteousness will bring peace. Yes, it will bring quietness and confidence forever. My people will live in safety, quietly at home. They will be at rest. Even if the forest should be destroyed and the city torn down,
Isaiah 32:17-19, NLT

Now declare today:

- I am the righteousness of God in Christ Jesus. Therefore, sickness, drop off of me now.
- Because I am the righteousness of God in Christ, I regain my sight today.
- Because I am the righteousness of God in Christ, doors will open to me this week. Every closed door, be opened!
- Because I am the righteousness of God in Christ, I receive divine connections.
- Because I am the righteousness of God in Christ Jesus, I have victory over sin, over bad habits, over weaknesses of the flesh, and over anger—all in Jesus' name. Amen!

Ruling Your World

Yes, when you start unlocking unlimited wonders in Christ, you can start *Ruling Your World!*

Chapter 7

Walking in the Miraculous

As the women were on their way, some of the guards went into the city and told the leading priests what had happened. A meeting with the elders was called, and they decided to give the soldiers a large bribe. They told the soldiers, "You must say, 'Jesus' disciples came during the night while we were sleeping, and they stole his body.' If the governor hears about it, we'll stand up for you so you won't get in trouble." So the guards accepted the bribe and said what they were told to say. Their story spread widely among the Jews, and they still tell it today.

                                        Matthew 28:11-15, NLT

Imagine, people were paid to discredit the truth that Jesus was alive. In the same way, the life of miracles today is not just about healings and experiencing the supernatural; it's about Jesus Christ, the Son of God, and the proof that He is alive and is the same yesterday, today, and forever. The world is confused and does not seem to know this truth. The working of miracles and wonders by Jesus' followers is the proof:

> *During the forty days after he suffered and died, he appeared to the apostles from time to time, and he proved to them in many ways that he was actually alive. And he talked to them about the Kingdom of God.* Acts 1:3, NLT

If Jesus is alive, there must be infallible proof, and I am sent by God to provide that infallible proof. He has conquered, and the battle for your destiny is over. Get yourself in line with this truth:

> *And you know that God anointed Jesus of Nazareth with the Holy Spirit and with power. Then Jesus went around doing good and healing all who were oppressed by the devil, for God was with him.* Acts 10:38, NLT

My assignment here today is simple. I am sent to declare that Jesus is alive and to prove it with my actions. Miracles and healings are demonstrations of God's love and compassion for mankind. He cannot stand for any of His children to be in chains or lacking anything they need:

> *Is there no medicine in Gilead?*
>   *Is there no physician there?*
> *Why is there no healing*
>   *for the wounds of my people?*
> Jeremiah 8:22, NKJV

In the midst of chaos and death, He said, "Let these go, that it might be fulfilled that I lost no one":

> *Jesus answered, I have told you that I am he: if therefore ye seek me, let these go their way: that the saying might be fulfilled, which he spake, Of them which thou gavest me have I lost none.*
>
> John 18:8-9

The Bible says that the Good Shepherd lays down His life for the sheep:

> *I am the good shepherd: the good shepherd giveth his life for the sheep.*
>
> John 10:11

> *But when he saw the multitudes, he was moved with compassion on them, because they fainted, and were scattered abroad, as sheep having no shepherd.*
>
> Matthew 9:36

Having compassion means that I can't stand something happening to a person when I have the power to prevent it. This was Jesus' demonstration of compassion for the needs of the people of His day—both materially and spiritually. He said, "No, it cannot happen." They were like sheep without a shepherd. A shepherd makes sure the sheep have the right pasture and never lack:

> *The LORD is my shepherd; I shall not want. He maketh me to lie down in green pastures: he leadeth me beside the still waters. He restoreth my soul: he leadeth me in the paths of righteousness for his name's sake. Yea, though I walk through the valley of the shadow of death, I will fear no evil: for thou art with me; thy rod and thy staff they comfort me. Thou preparest a table before me in the presence of mine enemies: thou anointest my head with oil; my cup runneth over.* Psalm 23:1-5

Get ready! Nothing will be left uncovered in Jesus' name. He has compassion on those in need:

> *And Jesus went forth, and saw a great multitude, and was moved with*

> *compassion toward them, and he healed their sick.* Matthew 14:14

Jesus had compassion on the sick, and the good news is that He is the same yesterday, today, and forever:

> *Jesus Christ the same yesterday, and to day, and for ever.* Hebrews 13:8

Jesus' ministry of healing was a natural part of His mission because He couldn't bear to see people suffer:

> *And the inhabitant shall not say, I am sick: the people that dwell therein shall be forgiven their iniquity.*
> Isaiah 33:24

When there is compassion, the only requirement is faith to receive what God is offering you. *"His compassions fail not"*:

> *It is of the* LORD's *mercies that we are not consumed, because his compassions*

> *fail not. They are new every morning: great is thy faithfulness.*
> Lamentations 3:22-23

No sickness can remain on you today because Jesus is the same yesterday, today, and forever:

> *And a great multitude followed him, because they saw his miracles which he did on them that were diseased.*
> John 6:2. KJV

He hasn't changed.

> *I say unto thee, Arise, and take up thy bed, and go thy way into thine house.*
> Mark 2:11

No, He hasn't changed.

> *Then Jesus saith unto them, Children, have ye any meat? They answered him, No. And he said unto them, Cast the net on the right side of the ship, and ye*

shall find. They cast therefore, and now they were not able to draw it for the multitude of fishes.

As soon then as they were come to land, they saw a fire of coals there, and fish laid thereon, and bread.

John 21:5-6 and 9

He hasn't changed.

Therefore we ought to give the more earnest heed to the things which we have heard, lest at any time we should let them slip. For if the word spoken by angels was stedfast, and every transgression and disobedience received a just recompence of reward; how shall we escape, if we neglect so great salvation; which at the first began to be spoken by the Lord, and was confirmed unto us by them that heard him ; God also bearing them witness, both with signs and wonders, and with divers miracles, and gifts of the Holy Ghost, according to his own will? Hebrews 2:1-4

He hasn't changed. His compassion is still unfailing:

> *But thou, O Lord, art a God full of compassion, and gracious, longsuffering, and plenteous in mercy and truth.*
> Psalm 86:15

> *He hath made his wonderful works to be remembered: the Lord is gracious and full of compassion.* Psalm 111:4

> *The Lord is gracious, and full of compassion; slow to anger, and of great mercy. The Lord is good to all: and his tender mercies are over all his works.* Psalm 145:8-9

Our God will do anything for you, even when you don't deserve it.

Everywhere Jesus went, He was moved with compassion, and miracles happened:

> *And Jesus, moved with compassion, put forth his hand, and touched him, and saith unto him, I will; be thou clean.*

> *And as soon as he had spoken, immediately the leprosy departed from him, and he was cleansed.* Mark 1:41-42

We connect to this divine compassion by faith through Jesus' name. His name contains His Person, His name is the proof that He is here and alive, and His name carries His authority and power. He said:

> *Verily, verily, I say unto you, He that believeth on me, the works that I do shall he do also; and greater works than these shall he do; because I go unto my Father. And whatsoever ye shall ask in my name, that will I do, that the Father may be glorified in the Son. If ye shall ask any thing in my name, I will do it.*
> John 14:12-14

The greater works we are to do will come through His name. Why?

> *And being found in fashion as a man, he humbled himself, and became obedient*

unto death, even the death of the cross. Wherefore God also hath highly exalted him, and given him a name which is above every name: that at the name of Jesus every knee should bow, of things in heaven, and things in earth, and things under the earth; and that every tongue should confess that Jesus Christ is Lord, to the glory of God the Father.
Philippians 2:8-11

The Lord is there with you, and His powerful name has not changed. At the Beautiful Gate, that name worked wonders:

Then Peter said, Silver and gold have I none; but such as I have give I thee: In the name of Jesus Christ of Nazareth rise up and walk. And he took him by the right hand, and lifted him up: and immediately his feet and ankle bones received strength. And he leaping up stood, and walked, and entered with them into the temple, walking, and leaping, and praising God. And all the

> *people saw him walking and praising God: and they knew that it was he which sat for alms at the Beautiful gate of the temple: and they were filled with wonder and amazement at that which had happened unto him.*
>
> Acts 3:6-10

Whatever is crippled in your life is receiving strength right now in the name of Jesus Christ:

Here's another example:

> *And there he found a certain man named Aeneas, which had kept his bed eight years, and was sick of the palsy. And Peter said unto him, Aeneas, Jesus Christ maketh thee whole: arise, and make thy bed. And he arose immediately.* Acts 9:33-34

Jesus is there with you today. All you have to do is ask in His name. He is there by your side to get the job done for *"whosoever will."* His Word declares:

> *And it shall come to pass, that whosoever shall call on the name of the Lord shall be saved.* Acts 2:21

Call on the name of the Lord, and you shall be saved. Your salvation is today in Jesus' name. The life of Jesus is in that name. Take what you need now by faith in Jesus' name.

You cannot miss your greatness in the days ahead. It has been predetermined and established based upon God's divine covenant. When covenant is involved, you can rest in total conviction that it will be done.

God said He would never break His covenant:

> *Thus saith the LORD; If ye can break my covenant of the day, and my covenant of the night, and that there should not be day and night in their season ...*
> *Thus saith the LORD; If my covenant be not with day and night, and if I have not appointed the ordinances of heaven and earth ...* Jeremiah 33:20 and 25. KJV

The intention of God is to bless you, never to hurt you. If you live in fear, it may mean that you don't know His heart. The people of Israel thought God took them into the wilderness to kill them and that He had given them commandments to destroy them. The truth was that all He did was to bless them:

An altar of earth thou shalt make unto me, and shalt sacrifice thereon thy burnt offerings, and thy peace offerings, thy sheep, and thine oxen: in all places where I record my name I will come unto thee, and I will bless thee. And if thou wilt make me an altar of stone, thou shalt not build it of hewn stone: for if thou lift up thy tool upon it, thou hast polluted it. Exodus 20:24-25

In the same way, God sent Jesus to bless you, not to condemn you:

Unto you first God, having raised up his Son Jesus, sent him to bless you, in turning away every one of you from his iniquities. Acts 3:26

We now have an Advocate, an attorney, who stands to plead our case and has never lost a battle:

> *My little children, these things write I unto you, that ye sin not. And if any man sin, we have an advocate with the Father, Jesus Christ the righteous.*
> 1 John 2:1

The job of an attorney is to get you out of the problem before a judge. God is the Judge, and Jesus is your Attorney. I repeat: the good news is that He has never lost a case:

> *I, even I, am he that blotteth out thy transgressions for mine own sake, and will not remember thy sins. Put me in remembrance: let us plead together: declare thou, that thou mayest be justified.* Isaiah 43:25-26

God wants to bless you. That's why He sent us a Savior. That Savior said that He used the *"key of David"* to open doors, and that no man could shut them:

> *He that hath an ear, let him hear what the Spirit saith unto the churches. And to the angel of the church in Philadelphia write; These things saith he that is holy, he that is true, he that hath the key of David, he that openeth, and no man shutteth; and shutteth, and no man openeth.* Revelation 3:6-7

It is your turn to get the keys and take over. Jesus told Peter:

> *And I will give unto thee the keys of the kingdom of heaven: and whatsoever thou shalt bind on earth shall be bound in heaven: and whatsoever thou shalt loose on earth shall be loosed in heaven.*
> Matthew 16:19

Knowing that the keys are your access to greatness, let's think about some important keys:

THE KEY OF CONSECRATION AND COMMITMENT

You won't need to scream and shout at any door if you're holding the key to it. Every man's glory is in his story. When you know the story, you will walk in the glory.

David's heart of commitment to God's Kingdom knocked out every adversary standing at his doors. He said:

> *For a day in thy courts is better than a thousand. I had rather be a doorkeeper in the house of my God, than to dwell in the tents of wickedness.*
> Psalm 84:10, NKJV

> *One thing have I desired of the LORD, that will I seek after; that I may dwell in the house of the LORD all the days of my life, to behold the beauty of the LORD, and to enquire in his temple.* Psalm 27:4

> *As the hart panteth after the water brooks, so panteth my soul after thee, O God. My soul thirsteth for God, for*

> *the living God: when shall I come and appear before God?* Psalm 42:1-2

David's heart was in the right place, and because of that, God vowed to him:

> *Once have I sworn by my holiness that I will not lie unto David. His seed shall endure for ever, and his throne as the sun before me. It shall be established for ever as the moon, and as a faithful witness in heaven. Selah.*
> Psalm 89:35-37

In David, God found a man after His own heart, a man who would fulfill His will:

> *And when he had removed him* [King Saul], *he raised up unto them David to be their king; to whom also he gave their testimony, and said, I have found David the son of Jesse, a man after mine own heart, which shall fulfil all my will.*
> Acts 13:22

Jesus said:

> *(For after all these things do the Gentiles seek:) for your heavenly Father knoweth that ye have need of all these things. But seek ye first the kingdom of God, and his righteousness; and all these things shall be added unto you.*
> Matthew 6:32-33

That's the key!

> *Those that be planted in the house of the LORD shall flourish in the courts of our God.* Psalm 92:13

Where are you planted? That's the key!

> *Beloved, now are we the sons of God, and it doth not yet appear what we shall be: but we know that, when he shall appear, we shall be like him; for we shall see him as he is. And every man that hath this hope in him purifieth himself, even as he is pure.* 1 John 3:2-3

What does this mean by *"purifieth himself"*? It means he separates himself, consecrating and committing himself to God. That's an important key. Until God becomes number one in our lives, we will never have a position on Earth.

THE KEY OF AUTHORITY AND POWER

> *And I will give unto thee the keys of the kingdom of heaven: and whatsoever thou shalt bind on earth shall be bound in heaven: and whatsoever thou shalt loose on earth shall be loosed in heaven.* Matthew 16:19

David's major strength was understanding God's divine presence with him always, no matter what confronted him. Because he was so sure that the presence of God with him would always bring the answer he needed, he could sing:

> *Yea, though I walk through the valley of the shadow of death, I will fear no evil: for thou art with me; thy rod and thy staff they comfort me.* Psalm 23:4

Everyone experiences valleys, but the valley of the shadow of death refers to a terminal case unless God is there with you. The purpose God had in mind for every man and woman on the Earth was to rule, to dominate the world. David saw this and said:

> *What is man, that thou art mindful of him? and the son of man, that thou visitest him? For thou hast made him a little lower than the angels, and hast crowned him with glory and honour. Thou madest him to have dominion over the works of thy hands; thou hast put all things under his feet.*
>
> Psalm 8:4-6

This was why everything bowed to David. He could sing with confidence:

> *When the wicked, even mine enemies and my foes, came upon me to eat up my flesh, they stumbled and fell. Though an host should encamp*

> *against me, my heart shall not fear: though war should rise against me, in this will I be confident.* Psalm 27:2-3

David's awareness of the divine presence gave him authority and power. Jesus said that he had *"the key of David,"* and nothing could stop Him. He declared, *"I and my Father are one,"* (John 10:30).

To Philip, He said:

> *Have I been so long time with you, and yet hast thou not known me, Philip? he that hath seen me hath seen the Father; and how sayest thou then, Show us the Father?* John 14:9

This was the key to unstoppable results in Jesus' ministry. Now this key is with you. Jesus said so:

> *Teaching them to observe all things whatsoever I have commanded you: and, lo, I am with you always, even unto the end of the world. Amen.* Matthew 28:20

> *Let your conversation be without covetousness; and be content with such things as ye have: for he hath said, I will never leave thee, nor forsake thee.*
> Hebrews 13:5

God is with me, Love is with me, and Love never fails. This is an important key.

The Key of Death and Hades

Because of the finished work of Jesus, death no longer has the final say for any believer. The death-dealing power of Satan was completely taken away at the resurrection of our Lord Jesus. When He gave up the ghost, Satan lost the key. The Bible says:

> *When Jesus therefore had received the vinegar, he said, It is finished: and he bowed his head, and gave up the ghost.*
> John 19:30

What does that mean?

> *Forasmuch then as the children are partakers of flesh and blood, he also himself likewise took part of the same; that through death he might destroy him that had the power of death, that is, the devil; and deliver them who through fear of death were all their lifetime subject to bondage.*
>
> Hebrews 2:14-15

By reason of His death, Jesus destroyed the power of the devil. The powers of darkness regretted that day. If they had known what would happen, *"they would not have crucified the Lord of glory"*:

> *Which none of the princes of this world knew: for had they known it, they would not have crucified the Lord of glory.*
>
> 1 Corinthians 2:8

> *So when this corruptible shall have put on incorruption, and this mortal shall have put on immortality, then shall be brought to pass the saying that is written, Death is swallowed up in victory.*
>
> 1 Corinthians 15:54

David saw it and used it. He sang:

> *With long life will I satisfy him, and shew him my salvation.* Psalm 91:16

> *I shall not die, but live, and declare the works of the LORD.* Psalm 118:17

This man saw into God's plan of redemption. Jesus confirmed it:

> *I am he that liveth, and was dead; and, behold, I am alive for evermore, Amen; and have the keys of hell and of death.*
> Revelation 1:18

He is now extending this key to you. Use it boldly. How? Stop speaking death. *"Death and life are in the power of the tongue":*

> *Death and life are in the power of the tongue: and they that love it shall eat the fruit thereof.* Proverbs 18:21

Solomon was not a lucky man, as you might suppose. He heard these truths from his father and learned them well. He later wrote:

> *My son, hear the instruction of thy father, and forsake not the law of thy mother: for they shall be an ornament of grace unto thy head, and chains about thy neck.* Proverbs 1:8-9

We are going forward today by the power and the anointing of the Holy Spirit in the name of Jesus Christ.

Death is a guarantee that the benefactors will now have access to the inheritance. The will is not mature until the death of the testator. That is why Moses would kill an animal and use its blood as a proof of death for access. The blood of Jesus is proof that our inheritance is now mature, and we can receive the benefits of His will.

We have the most powerful team ever working with us in the new covenant, helping us win at all costs. Besides God the Father, Son, and Holy Ghost, we are surrounded by myriads of angels who excel in strength. They are our ministers and will make sure no stone or obstacles set by the enemy stops us. They always carry us in their hands so that we don't dash our feet against a stone.

Our heavenly Father Himself is the Righteous Judge, Jesus is our Advocate, Intercessor, Mediator and Savior, and therefore our justification is established. No matter what ails us, we can get to the blood, repent, and receive forgiveness, and by the righteousness of God, become one with Him instantly.

With that, Satan and all his cohorts have a problem. Because we are the righteousness of God in Christ Jesus, he must take his hands off of us. He cannot lay claim to anything that Jesus has already paid for.

When we judge things by their physical appearance alone, we will miss the whole content. The greatest strength of a believer is to distinguish between what is eternal and what is temporal. Paul wrote:

> *While we look not at the things which are seen, but at the things which are not seen: for the things which are seen are temporal; but the things which are not seen are eternal.* 2 Corinthians 4:18

Things that are seen are temporal, and things that are not seen are eternal. The Bible, the Word of God, is eternal:

> *The grass withereth, the flower fadeth: but the word of our God shall stand for ever.* Isaiah 40:8

This is what controls the temporal. If something is seen or within the ability of the senses, the eternal Word of God can change it. This is what Jesus was saying:

> *I know thy works: behold, I have set before thee an open door, and no man can shut it: for thou hast a little strength, and hast kept my word, and hast not denied my name. Behold, I will make them of the synagogue of Satan, which say they are Jews, and are not, but do*

lie; behold, I will make them to come and worship before thy feet, and to know that I have loved thee. Revelation 3:8-9

What an important key!

The Key of Righteousness and Grace

One of the most powerful keys in the hand of Jesus was the key of righteousness:

Thou lovest righteousness, and hatest wickedness: therefore God, thy God, hath anointed thee with the oil of gladness above thy fellows. Psalm 45:7

Righteousness gives us the ability to stand before God as if our sin had never existed. This opens any door at any time because righteousness exalts and is a ruling force. You are accepted by God to do all you desire according to His will.

David understood that righteousness comes from God and not from our own efforts. He went into the temple and ate the shewbread which was forbidden except for the priests, and he escaped punishment. He said:

> *Therefore the L*ORD *hath recompensed me according to my righteousness; according to my cleanness in his eye sight.* 2 Samuel 22:25

It is not "according to my righteousness in [my] sight," but in His:

> *And in thy majesty ride prosperously because of truth and meekness and righteousness; and thy right hand shall teach thee terrible things.* Psalm 45:4

God confirmed this:

> *And rent the kingdom away from the house of David, and gave it thee: and yet thou hast not been as my servant David, who kept my commandments, and who followed me with all his heart, to do that only which was right in mine eyes.* 1 Kings 14:8

David's righteousness was not based on the Law but on faith in the love of God. He (David) violated the Law on multiple occasions. He was an adulterer (see 2 Samuel 11:4), a murderer (see 2 Samuel 11:15), was prideful (see 1 Chronicles 21:1, 7, 8), and was a negligent father (see 1 Kings 1:6). His sins caused great pain and anguish for himself, his family, and the nation. We know that God was aware of David's sin and He cannot lie (see Romans 4:6). Still, David sang:

> *Blessed is the man unto whom the Lord imputeth not iniquity, and in whose spirit there is no guile.* Psalm 32:3

We also know that God could not simply overlook the sins of David because of who David was. How, then, could God refer to David as someone who did only what was right? It was David's connection to Jesus:

> *Have mercy upon me, O God, according to thy lovingkindness: according unto the multitude of thy tender mercies blot out my transgressions. Wash me throughly from mine iniquity, and cleanse me from my sin.* Psalm 51:1-2

This was the key to his righteousness:

> *If thou, Lord, shouldest mark iniquities, O LORD, who shall stand? But there is forgiveness with thee, that thou mayest be feared.* Psalm 130:3-4

> *For if by one man's offence death reigned by one; much more they which receive abundance of grace and of the gift of righteousness shall reign in life by one, Jesus Christ.* Romans 5:17

Yes, this is an important key.

THE KEY OF DIVINE GUIDANCE AND DIRECTION

Beloved, success and breakthrough are legal for a child of God, but attaining that success is another thing entirely:

> *The LORD shall open unto thee his good treasure, the heaven to give the rain unto thy land in his season, and to bless all the work of thine hand: and thou shalt lend unto many nations, and thou shalt not borrow. And the LORD shall make thee the head, and not the tail; and thou shalt be above only, and thou shalt not be beneath; if that thou hearken unto the commandments of the LORD thy God, which I command thee this day, to observe and to do them.*
> Deuteronomy 28:12-13

> *Christ hath redeemed us from the curse of the law, being made a curse for us: for it is written, Cursed is every one that hangeth on a tree: that the blessing of Abraham might come on the Gentiles through Jesus Christ; that we might receive the promise of the Spirit through faith.* Galatians 3:13-14

The Bible says:

> *The labour of the foolish wearieth every one of them, because he knoweth not how to go to the city.* Ecclesiastes 10:15

It takes direction to attain results. The children of Israel knew they were going to a land flowing with milk and honey, but they were discouraged because they didn't know how to get there. To solve the mystery, God led them through the wilderness:

> *For the LORD's portion is his people; Jacob is the lot of his inheritance. He found him in a desert land, and in the waste howling wilderness; he led him about, he instructed him, he kept him as the apple of his eye.*
> Deuteronomy 32:9-10

One of the greatest privileges of the redeemed is to be led of the Lord in every situation. If you ask God for His guidance and are willing to follow, He will show you the way:

> *Thus saith the* LORD, *thy Redeemer, the Holy One of Israel; I am the* LORD *thy God which teacheth thee to profit, which leadeth thee by the way that thou shouldest go.* Isaiah 48:17

> *For as many as are led by the Spirit of God, they are the sons of God.* Romans 8:14

As a child of God, there is a witness within you. David asked God, "Shall I pursue?" and God answered, "Yes." At other times, God said no. Jesus was led by watching to see what His Father was doing:

> *I have many things to say and to judge of you: but he that sent me is true; and I speak to the world those things which I have heard of him. They understood not that he spake to them of the Father. Then said Jesus unto them, When ye have lifted up the Son of man, then*

> *shall ye know that I am he, and that I do nothing of myself; but as my Father hath taught me, I speak these things.*
> John 8:26-28

You cannot afford to jump into things without divine guidance, for you are limited in knowledge about the future:

> *There is a way which seemeth right unto a man, but the end thereof are the ways of death.* Proverbs 14:12

Ask God first. Then pray in the Holy Ghost. There will be an inspiration or a sort of nudge. Follow it by faith without wavering. If God can lead a donkey, you are much more qualified. This is an important key.

THE KEY OF FAITH

Faith is not a religious language; it is Kingdom language. It is the currency that buys everything in the Kingdom of God. Jesus said:

If thou canst believe, all things are possible to him that believeth.   Mark 9:23

Faith is a conviction based on the Word of God. You cannot ever have faith if you don't know that the Almighty God who created all things is for you. You cannot have more faith in things that are created than you do in the Creator Himself. He said:

But without faith it is impossible to please Him, for he who comes to God must believe that He is, and that He is a rewarder of those who diligently seek Him.   Hebrews 11:6, NKJV

When you believe, the most powerful throne in the Universe backs you up. God doesn't do this because you deserve it; He does it because He loves you.

God's Word is not just another sermon or an encouraging story. It is His will, and it contains His plans for you, an expression of His love. What you read in the Scriptures is a love letter from your heavenly Dad, and it must come to pass, for the integrity of the Almighty is attached to it.

The key of David works every time because it is based on faith in God's Word. David said:

> *I would have lost heart, unless I had believed*
> *That I would see the goodness of the* Lord
> *In the land of the living.*
> Psalm 27:13, NKJV

No one could stand against the size and strength of Goliath until David came along. You may have faith but never release it to God. Instead, you release it to the devil because of the fear he taught you. God gave you love, power, and a sound mind, but you learned fear from others. But if God says you have the keys, then you have them.

God is no fool. He knows that you lack strength in yourself:

> *I know thy works: behold, I have set before thee an open door, and no man can shut it: for thou hast a little strength, and hast kept my word, and hast not denied my name.* Revelation 3:8

Even then, He loves you. The diciples wondered:

> *And he was in the hinder part of the ship, asleep on a pillow: and they awake him, and say unto him, Master, carest thou not that we perish?* Mark 4:38

"Don't You care?" they asked. They called Him Master. They also called Him Lord, and yet they thought they were perishing and that He didn't care:

> *Then His disciples came to Him and awoke Him, saying, "Lord, save us! We are perishing!"* Matthew 8:25, NKJV

Luke also recorded this story:

> *And they came to Him and awoke Him,*

> *saying, "Master, Master, we are perishing!" Then He arose and rebuked the wind and the raging of the water. And they ceased, and there was a calm.*
> Luke 8:24, NKJV

When Jesus heard that Lazarus, His friend, was sick, He told the disciples:

> *This sickness is not unto death, but for the glory of God, that the Son of God may be glorified through it.*
> John 11:4, NKJV

The next thing they knew, the man was dead and buried. Obviously Jesus knew something they didn't know.

When they got there, several days had passed. Everyone was weeping and mourning. They said Lazarus' body must already be smelling bad. Jesus knew something they didn't.

Today we know what eventually happened. Lazarus was raised to life again, and Jesus was proved right. It was not over until it was over. Things are changing now for you too.

The Lord cannot give you more than your ability to receive. Have faith in God! His supply is never ending. The work was finished from the foundation of the world:

> *For only we who believe can enter his rest. As for the others, God said,*
> *"In my anger I took an oath:*
> *'They will never enter my place of rest,'" even though this rest has been ready since he made the world. We know it is ready because of the place in the Scriptures where it mentions the seventh day: "On the seventh day God rested from all his work."*
>
> Hebrews 4:3-4, NLT

It is finished, but the receiving of the finished work is a daily affair that must be done by faith.

There is a mystery behind the veil of the Temple in Jerusalem that was torn from top to bottom at Jesus' resurrection. God gave the design for this veil,

Ruling Your World

or curtain, through Moses. Behind the veil was something all Israel waited for every time the High Priest went inside, and he did it only once a year. This was the place of God's presence, and so no one else could go there.

When the High Priest went in, he never went alone. He was always going with a blood sacrifice. And when he came out, he never came out alone. He always carried with him the blessing of God for the people:

*Then the L*ORD *said to Moses, "Tell Aaron and his sons to bless the people of Israel with this special blessing:*

*'May the L*ORD *bless you*
　and protect you.
*May the L*ORD *smile on you*
　and be gracious to you.
*May the L*ORD *show you his favor*
　and give you his peace.'

Whenever Aaron and his sons bless the people of Israel in my name, I myself will bless them." Numbers 6:22-27, NLT

Everyone was waiting for this blessing when the High Priest came out from the presence of the Lord that resided inside the Most Holy Place. It was not because of the man, but what rested upon the man.

After the resurrection of Jesus, the priesthood changed. It was no longer Aaron and his descendants. A new Priest after the order of Melchizedek had come, not by the Law but by divine appointment.

> *And the psalmist pointed this out when he prophesied,*
> *"You are a priest forever in the order of Melchizedek."*
> *Yes, the old requirement about the priesthood was set aside because it was weak and useless. For the law never made anything perfect. But now we have confidence in a better hope, through which we draw near to God.*
> *This new system was established with*

> *a solemn oath. Aaron's descendants became priests without such an oath, but there was an oath regarding Jesus. For God said to him,*
> *"The Lord has taken an oath and will not break his vow:*
> *'You are a priest forever.'"*
> Hebrews 7:17-21, NLT

It was not the Roman soldiers who executed Jesus; He died at the hand of the High Priest. And when He did, He removed forever the veil of the Temple, tearing it apart, ripping it from top to bottom, exposing the presence of a holy God to all who would enter.

Heaven is opened to you. Claim your blessing.

The priesthood of Jesus is after the order of Melchizedek, not after the order of Aaron. But what was the difference?

> *[Melchizedek king of Salem (ancient Jerusalem) brought out bread and wine [for them]; he was the priest of God Most*

> *High. And Melchizedek blessed Abram and said,*
> *"Blessed (joyful, favored) be Abram by God Most High,*
> *Creator and Possessor of heaven and earth;*
> *And blessed, praised, and glorified be God Most High,*
> *Who has given your enemies into your hand."*
> *And Abram gave him a tenth of all [the treasure he had taken in battle]. The king of Sodom said to Abram, "Give me the people and keep the goods (spoils of battle) for yourself."* **Genesis 14:18-21, AMP**

Melchisedec blessed Abraham, giving him the key to Heaven and Earth:

> *(as it is written [in Scripture], "I have made you a father of many nations") in the sight of Him in whom he believed, that is, God who gives life to the dead and calls into being that which does not exist.* **Romans 4:17, AMP**

This was not because Abraham had paid tithes; it was grace in action. The tithe was just the proof that Abraham was blessed. If you are not tithing, you are telling God He didn't bless you, that He lied, and therefore you are not honoring Him:

> *He who has an ear, let him hear and heed what the Spirit says to the churches.*
> *And to the angel (divine messenger) of the church in Philadelphia write:*
> *"These are the words of the Holy One, the True One, He who has the key [to the house] of David, He who opens and no one will [be able to] shut, and He who shuts and no one opens.*
>
> Revelation 3:6-7, AMP

Jesus is now our High Priest forever after the order of Melchizedek, and He keeps on blessing us all the time. Our access to everything in the Kingdom is through Jesus. He holds the key:

> *And being found in fashion as a man, he*

humbled himself, and became obedient unto death, even the death of the cross. Wherefore God also hath highly exalted him, and given him a name which is above every name: that at the name of Jesus every knee should bow, of things in heaven, and things in earth, and things under the earth.
Philippians 2:8-10

Who is gone into heaven, and is on the right hand of God; angels and authorities and powers being made subject unto him. 1 Peter 3:22

Now, it's our time to reign on the Earth. This great High Priest has entered into the Heavens and with His sacrifice appeased God. Now we can come boldly based on His works and not our own:

So then, since we have a great High Priest who has entered heaven, Jesus the Son of God, let us hold firmly to what we believe. This High Priest of

> *ours understands our weaknesses, for he faced all of the same testings we do, yet he did not sin. So let us come boldly to the throne of our gracious God. There we will receive his mercy, and we will find grace to help us when we need it most.*
> Hebrews 4:14-16, NLT

Yes, when you start walking in the miraculous, you can start *Ruling Your World*!

Other Books by Dr. Abiola Idowu

HEAVEN on EARTH

Bishop Dr. Abiola Idowu

WALKING AND LIVING IN YOUR INHERITANCE

BISHOP ABIOLA IDOWU

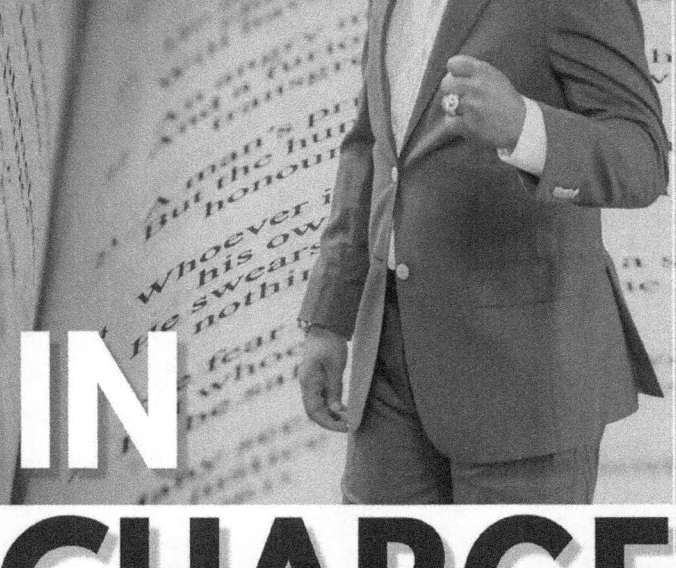

Author Contact Information

You may contact the author directly in the following way:

eMail: Bishopidowu@crepa.org

Telephone: (904) 469-5724

www.ingramcontent.com/pod-product-compliance
Lightning Source LLC
Chambersburg PA
CBHW030915090426
42737CB00007B/199